Very short bio!

There was a time in my life when I felt as you might well be feeling today. I had quite a tough childhood, with some not-so-healthy mental and emotional abuse. I went on to attract a partner who gave me more of the same, and I was bullied for 10 years by my boss at work. So as you can see, I was far from living the life of my dreams!

The problem was that I felt completely powerless and didn't realise that I could actually do anything about what was happening to me. I just thought this was the nature of life; you had to grin and bear it and take the good times when they came along as little oases of respite.

What I hadn't realised back then is that it's the good times that you should be having **most of the time**, and not the other way around.

It got to the stage where I had been depressed for many years, but then it got even deeper (the "dark night of the soul") and I realised that if I didn't do something about my life, then I was probably going to end it.

I started reading – loads! I went to therapy for five years; then I went back to school and became a psychotherapist. **YUP**, I needed an overdose of it.

What I learnt through my reading and my studies changed everything for me and now I'm offering all of that learning to you without any of the hassle. It's actually really easy when you finally get going; and the relief of feeling you and your life change so quickly will give you the confirmation and confidence you were looking for to keep up the momentum.

I call the information which you'll find in this book the "five techniques to get empowered," because these are what I put into place to turn my life around. I used to think that life was happening "at" me, that there was **nothing** I could do to change or influence it, but I couldn't have been more wrong (thankfully). Adopting these five ways of being into my life totally transformed it - and I'm sure they can help change your life too.

This has to be the best-kept secret on the planet today: when you take back real responsibility for yourself, when you start being aware of your personal power and giving yourself what you need in order to thrive, then you **literally can build the life that you want.**

I have done it, my friends who wanted to have done it, and my clients are putting it into practice every day. I hope that with the ideas and examples you find in this book, you'll soon change your life too if that's what you want.

So let's get on with it already! You've been waiting long enough, and the brand new you is waiting in the wings.

Here's to having the life you desire. It is possible.

Amanda

Contents

Very short bio! 4

Introduction 8
   Re-Defining "Happy" 10
   5 chapters, 5 huge steps for humankind! 13

Chapter 1 - Boundaries; not barriers 14
   Boundaries and dysfunction 16
   Where do bad boundaries come from? 19
   What should you look for? 21
   How to start setting up your boundaries 26
   How to do it examples 30

Chapter 2 - Needs and wants; but not the brattish kind 34
   Needs versus Wants 37
   What are legitimate needs? 40
   Finding your needs 45
   Meeting your needs 47
   How to do it examples 53

Chapter 3 - Feelings; but without the pain 56
   What are feelings? 57
   Are you in touch with your feelings? 65
   How to be in touch with your feelings 67
   Feelings and how to influence them 72
   How to do it examples 74

Chapter 4 - Inner critic: who is that person in my head? 78

Identifying the Inner Critic 80
The wrath of the critic.. 83
Silencing Your Inner Critic 90
How to do it examples.. 94

Chapter 5 - Self-esteem: oh, I remember that! 99

Where does low self-esteem come from? 100
How low self-esteem affects your life 104
Low self-esteem and relationships 108
Building Up Your Self-Esteem 114
How to do it examples.. 118

Conclusion 123

Introduction

Helping ourselves or maybe even having therapy is just like anything else: if you bite off more than you can chew at any one time, then you won't be able to keep it all under control in your mouth, and you'll start dribbling. And nobody wants a dribbler!

Maybe your life is actually not too bad, thank you very much, but if you thought about it you could just "tweak" a couple of things to make it even better. However, because life is actually treating you fairly well, you may think that doing anything about the bits that could benefit from some improvement just seems like way too much effort. You probably think there's no point in rocking a boat that's floating anyway!

Or maybe your life is more complicated and you could really do with some proper therapy; not just talking to friends or family and getting advice. But therapy can seem very

as a concept to some people. Some of you may be put off by the time commitment, or there could be a stigma attached to going, or you might think it's pointless as it won't make a difference. As a result, many of us prefer to shrug our shoulders and carry on with our less-than-satisfying life rather than think we can do something about it. There seems to be a big emotional hole that opens up at the thought of going to see someone... it might make you feel tired before you even get started, or uncomfortable, or defensive - or maybe even angry.

However, what you might not have realised is that just because your life isn't giving you what you need right now, it doesn't mean that it has to remain that way. You can make a few changes without sinking the boat and if you've got bigger problems, you certainly don't have to go and spill the beans to another person in order to get things shifting. You might find sharing your deepest thoughts and emotions with someone else too difficult, or you might just plain not be able to afford it. This is a book which can offer you the comfort and safety of making the changes you want, in bite-sized pieces and with no pressure from anyone, especially not your bank manager! It is actually possible to change your life with ease and without disturbance: *you can do it painlessly, and fast.*

The pages of this book contain the ultimate in user-friendly psychobabble. I will explain why incorporating the 5 techniques which I recommend into your way of being will **definitely** transform your life. These techniques are the foundations for living a life that offers you proper happiness, and a real sense of being in charge of what you get out of it. You will go from feeling that there is nothing you can really control, to seeing things change in you, and around you, as you start giving yourself the proper grounding in self-care and respect. For many of us this might seem daunting or unrealistic, but it really isn't.

To make the information clear and totally useable I've also included everyday examples based on other people's experiences (it's always good to know you're not alone!) and of course, you'll have step by step guidance to clarify what to put into place and how to do it.

Re-Defining "Happy"

Many of us won't have had the childhood that we would have liked, but often we don't allow ourselves to measure the impact that this might've had on us and how we see and place ourselves in relation to the rest of the world. Our thoughts are shaped according to the messages we receive from our earliest childhood days. If we grew up in a family which was loving and happy then we would be much more likely to have confidence in life and what it had to offer us. This early message might see us through the whole of our lives, or with the different experiences we might've had, we may have then begun to lose faith in what life had to offer us and come to accept and expect receiving less than what we really need in order to thrive.

If we grew up in a family that was dysfunctional or where the dynamics between certain members were less than satisfactory, then we will have subconsciously constructed a set of beliefs about life that will affect us as adults. We are influenced by everything that surrounds us as children and we can't help but assimilate all the information we receive as being "acceptable" and "normal", even if it wasn't. If, for instance we were in an environment where the adults were abusive to us or each other, or where the familial interaction between parents and children or between siblings was unhealthy, then we would be more inclined to expect poor treatment of ourselves as adults, or to act negligently towards our own Self. The negative programming doesn't even necessarily have to have come from within your family. It might also have been brought to you through contact with other adults or children with whom you spent time as you were growing up.

The effect of all of these invisible influences is rarely assessed by us, but as a result you will probably have grown to adulthood with a multitude of exterior influences which will have (consciously, or most likely unconsciously) coloured your beliefs about what your expectations of life should be. These thoughts play a huge role in our way of being. They determine whether we assume that life will bring us a great number of events, people and circumstances that will essentially make us happy, empowered and thriving; or on the contrary, whether we experience life as painful, often complicated, and unfulfilling.

However, just because that's how it is at the moment doesn't mean that it has to stay that way.

Change is possible, despite the adversity we might encounter from everyday challenges such as our relationships, work, money, sickness, loneliness, depression...

If you are fed up with living a life that isn't satisfying, or happy, or content, then this book is the way forward. Your life should be full of laughter, good times and fulfilment on all levels: **yes**, that does include your relationships, your job and daily life. Happiness isn't just for the holidays!

If you want quick change but want to do it for yourself, in your own time, on your own terms, then this book is for you. It will completely change how you feel about yourself and how you function.

- You will start feeling great all the time.

- You will rediscover your worth as a person.
- Your confidence levels will explode.
- Your self-esteem will skyrocket.
- You will give to yourself as generously as you probably already give to others.
- You will no longer feel put down or undervalued.
- You will start to view life with trust and positivity.
- You will find that others start treating you with greater care, respect and love.
- You will feel powerful and in charge.
- You will be aware of what really works for you and how to fill your life with it.
- Your levels of contentment will rise.
- You will begin to feel truly, deeply happy.

As you change, get more energy, experience more hope and start to feel amazing, you'll see that you attract more positive people and experiences into your life. Everything just seems to get an automatic upgrade.

In 5 chapters' time, you will be well on your way to getting the life of your dreams…

Gone will be the days when you felt bad, or powerless, or victimised. You won't feel unheard, or let down, or just downright miserable a lot of the time. You're going to take control of this baby and change your life!

Yes, it all starts with YOU!

This book is all about saying me, **me**, **me** (well, I mean you, **you**, **you!**)

Oh, and despite the light-hearted tone I haven't forgotten this is serious; but life can be crappy enough, so dealing with it and creating change might as well be fun!

5 chapters, 5 huge steps for humankind!

Your life will never be the same again.

Ta dah! Here they are, the five techniques you've been waiting for. You might have heard of them as some remote notion that only applies to other people. You mightn't have realised that you need them too, and that without them, you'll have trouble living a life of balance and serenity where you feel fulfilled. I'll help you understand what they really represent and why it's so necessary that you integrate them into your life. You won't believe the difference they'll make to you, and for you.

- Boundaries; not barriers
- Needs and wants; but not the brattish kind
- Feelings; but without the pain
- Inner critic: who is that person in my head?
- Self-Esteem: oh, I remember that!

Once you're familiar with them you will of course be using the techniques from all five chapters simultaneously, but so as to not overload you with information, I've put them in the order which worked for me. However, to begin with, please feel free to apply them in a way that feels good for you. You can work on one more than the others if that's what you feel you need to do, or you can start using them in a different order. It's up to you.

You decide. Believe it or not, you're the boss!

Chapter 1

Boundaries; not barriers

Boundaries are those things that are often mentioned when people start discussing what it means to be psychologically aware. The importance of boundaries cannot be emphasised enough. They protect you, they keep you cared for and respected... But guess what? Contrary to popular belief, it's not just up to others to recognise your boundaries: it's up to you as well!

People without healthy boundaries tend to look to others to make them feel better about themselves. Very often the subconscious contract is: "I need love, so if you love me, or approve of me, I'll start giving over some of my rights as a human being as compensation. I will keep giving to you and I'll accept it when you don't treat me properly..."

Sounds crazy, doesn't it, when you hear it said like that? But very often that's where giving up your personal power and boundaries leads to. When you enter into this type of unwritten contract, sooner or later you will find that you're both holding up your part of the agreement: you will no longer be getting the care and attention that you're entitled to and the other person will definitely be getting his (or her) end of the bargain from you!

Whoa, that sounds like a bad place to be, don't you think?

Unfortunately, in this type of relationship (whether it's a love relationship, a friendship, or even a colleague at work) although it might feel as though everyone is starting out with the same status, the person with flaky boundaries is the one who invariably winds up holding the short straw and who cannot understand why this keeps happening to them.

This scenario makes sense though, doesn't it? If you don't have defined boundaries, then people can push them, pull them, or even knock them over. You wind up accepting detrimental treatment and thinking there's very little you can do about it, as you're probably already quite used to these kinds of proceedings and think they're an inevitable part of your life. After a while, no matter what type of relationship you're looking at, this violation of your personal limits will come to be seen by you as tolerable behaviour and your already shaky boundaries will become even more so.

So what does the word boundary actually mean? Well, according to various dictionaries it's:

- Something which announces a border or limit.

This confirms that you **are** meant to have limits for what is acceptable to you, physically, emotionally and mentally.

There's another meaning for boundary and for some of you out there, this particular meaning will ring a (very hollow) bell, because you are living the polar opposite!

- Something (a line, fence, or border) which shows where one area ends and another one starts.

OR

- A point or limit at which two things (including human beings!) become separate.

Oops! How many of you are guilty of blurring that one? How many of you have unfortunately mistaken a "love" relationship for one of total fusion with the other person? Where you blended together with that person to such an extent that you no longer know where you end and they begin? Subsequently, in this type of relationship, it more often than not means that the emphasis is on taking care of their needs and well-being, while yours become more and more effaced.

∞∞∞∞∞

Boundaries and dysfunction

Many of us with ineffective boundaries come from dysfunctional families. We've grown used to having our needs and wants discounted, ignored, or just plain abused. As a result we're more likely to accept when someone doesn't honour our boundaries and starts treating us with insufficient respect or kindness. Even if it makes us mad as hell, we usually have absolutely no idea how to go about changing the situation.

For instance, if you've had the feeling for a while that something isn't right in one of your relationships but you can't really put your finger on it, then you're probably in a relationship that is damaging to you and you'd be right to heed your instincts.

If you're not yet clear about what could be considered an unhealthy relationship, I've prepared a list to give you some help at recognising them. Again, it's a sad fact of life that sometimes we're so used to crummy relationships, we're unable to recognise one when it's staring us in the face.

Have you found yourself in any of the following situations with your partner, boss, family member or a friend?

- You feel more relaxed if you help them to feel happy.
- You hold yourself responsible for what their mood is.
- You feel guilty if things don't turn out the way they say they want them to.
- You feel more comfortable when you're constantly with them.
- You do more than your fair share of everything.
- You bend over backwards to please, help or get things right for them.
- You ignore your own needs and feelings, but are very aware of theirs.
- You're attracted to their problems and like to solve them if you can.
- You rarely feel good enough and they help you feel that way, too.
- You put up with bad behaviour from them and are usually the first to find an excuse for it!

If (as is probable), you've found yourself nodding your head at more than one of the points in the checklist above, then it means you're more than likely to be suffering from a case of the *abominable Boundaries* and weren't even aware of it!

You might not ever have thought about boundaries before, but by now you're probably realising that possibly yours aren't as clear as they could be. So as to really reinforce their importance, I would like to help you find out what kind of impact not having defined boundaries might be causing on your well-being.

Do you recognise yourself in any of the examples below?

- Your self-esteem is suffering.
- Your confidence is shaky.
- Your satisfaction and serenity levels are low.
- You feel insecure about yourself and your circumstances.
- Your happiness relies on the other person / people being happy.
- When there is conflict or tension, you feel an overwhelming need to "fix" everything which makes you anxious or fearful.
- You feel empty when you're not with this person or when you're not getting on with them.
- You focus only on this relationship and your others are suffering as a result.
- You no longer really know who you are.

It's a little bit shocking, isn't it, to read the effect that unsteady boundaries can have on us? Recognising yourself in some of those points in the list above might come as an unpleasant surprise. I bet you never realised that your feeling bad all this time was actually a result of not putting into place solid boundaries? But don't worry, because as soon as you start recognising that there's a problem you can begin to do something about it! This can be one of those moments in life where you appreciate that what you took for granted as your daily reality is actually shared by millions of other people. Millions of us really are going through life receiving very little nurture from our relationships but feeling almost single-handedly responsible for the well-being of at least one other person. We must be mad!

The great news of course, is that all of this can change! The fact that so many people live the same thing means that it's not personal and happening only to you. It can be fixed. Once you understand what is going on, rather than living it unquestioningly, then you can get cracking and do something about it.

∞∞∞∞∞

Where do bad boundaries come from?

Not having good boundaries comes from getting the message when you were younger that it was okay to not be listened to, or to not have your feelings and needs heard and respected. This message is one which you then carry into your adult life and which means that you are always ready to give in when somebody starts pushing what should really be recognised as reasonable personal limits. After all, that's what you've always been shown that boundaries are for: to be pushed!

As we get into the other chapters, you'll begin to see how all of this is linked. For instance, if your feelings were valued when you were a child then you would've been given the message that they were important, as they would have been taken into account. As a result, when you were in a situation where someone wasn't respecting your feelings or boundaries, you wouldn't accept it. Your natural boundaries would make themselves felt and you would set the person straight or walk away.

Unfortunately, those of us who were not so lucky to be given this message early on tend to put up with the obvious disregard of their boundaries and leave themselves open for all sorts of mistreatment. We're also more likely to develop behaviours that aren't healthy.

I'll be going into more detail about this in the next few pages, but here's a list to jumpstart your understanding of how bad boundaries might be displayed as unhealthy behaviour:

1. Feeling the need to share a lot of personal information with someone you've just met.
2. Accepting to be touched, or touching someone else inappropriately. This can range from just simply rubbing an arm, or touching a baby bump, all the way to sexual misconduct.
3. Falling in love too easily and too intensely.
4. Having unprotected sex with people you've just met, or using sex as a method of control, or to get your own way.
5. Overriding your instincts about a person and their behaviour and accepting it when they don't treat you well.
6. Accepting unjust criticism or put downs as "just a part of life."
7. Thinking it's "normal" to not be listened to or met halfway.
8. Feeling that relationships are all about control and manipulation (yours or theirs).

You might be surprised by some of these, whilst others might seem more obvious. Even something like rubbing a stranger's arm without their consent could be seen as invading their personal space and is symbolic of not being aware of what good boundaries are.

∞∞∞∞∞

What should you look for?

In my experience, establishing good personal boundaries means you need to have them in three main areas: physical, mental and emotional. You really do want to have them in all three areas, since they work as a cohesive unit.

1. **Physical boundaries**

   As seen above, not having good physical boundaries means that they can be violated by others, or you might infringe upon someone else's without realising. After all, if you don't know when to protect your physical boundaries, it probably means that you don't know how to observe someone else's. It can also lead to sexual acting out or not being able to refuse inappropriate sexual advances from someone else.

   Maggie leant over to really get her point across and put her hand on Sue's knee for emphasis. Sue was not comfortable with this at all, but didn't know how to ask Maggie to stop.

   When Carl leant over to kiss Anne, she didn't want him to, but she had no idea how to say no. She let him do it even though it made her feel awful.

   Physical boundaries are also about giving off the right signals to protect your space, such as keeping your body language positive:

   - Holding your head high to show that you will not be cowed by your aggressive boss at work.
   - Not crossing your arms in defence, but standing straight and being clear about what you will not accept.
   - Smiling and staying relaxed because you know what your limits are.

2. **Mental boundaries**

There are two main forms of healthy mental boundaries. One is where we do not leave ourselves open to varying degrees of mental abuse (tone of voice, derogatory comments, undermining etc.) from others and are able to say when we feel that this might be the case. The other kind of boundary means that we acknowledge our thoughts and feelings and we give them the importance and validity they should have. With this type of boundary, we protect ourselves from being invalidated by someone else or by ourselves and this keeps our well-being levels higher.

> *Bernard was used to getting his own way by telling Eve that she was wrong and didn't know what she was talking about. Even though she knew he shouldn't talk to her that way, a part of Eve was used to overruling how she felt about this treatment, so she let him berate her.*

> *Nicole knew that if she continued nagging, Steve would give in. Steve was used to being manipulated and had stopped showing any resistance to it. He was too drained by the mind games to respond and request that Nicole not harass him.*

> *Although James knew he was tired, when his boss asked him to stay late at work to finish a report, he didn't want to disappoint her. She was good at insinuating that he wasn't very competent, and so he agreed to do the overtime. It made him feel depressed, as he felt invalidated and used.*

3. **Emotional boundaries**

When our emotions and feelings are healthy and we recognise them, then we don't get caught up in other people's emotions, we're more able to recognise what belongs to us that we should attend to, and what is someone else's "stuff" that they have to deal with. When others try to make us feel responsible for their state of mind, or we allow them to take out their state of mind on us, or we make ourselves responsible for positively boosting their emotions, then we need to work on our boundaries.

> *Lea would start to feel distressed if Lionel was tired or said he felt bad. She would start ruminating about how she could help him to feel better.*
>
> *Peter used to scream at Jane when he was hassled at work. He'd tell her that it was because she hadn't cooked a meal he actually wanted to eat that he was now completely stressed out. Jane started feeling bad and believed that she might be responsible for his stress, instead of listening to her real feelings which told her that it was because he wasn't handling his pressure at work successfully that he was treating her badly.*

As you can see in the scenarios above, the people involved were enduring situations in their relationships which were not healthy or acceptable, but were the result of their weak personal boundaries. Having good boundaries means that you know what your personal limits are. You send out the message that over and above a certain point, certain behaviour or acts towards you are no longer going to be tolerated. This keeps you safe and secure. A person who has good boundaries has a subconscious feeling of security because they know that they will keep themselves protected. Other people also subconsciously know that you have limits and they tend not to test them. If they do, they soon find out that you're not going to put up with it!

For instance: when someone says "no" to you and they mean it, you can hear it and you know that they're sincere; that they have set a clear limit. It's all in the tone of voice and the posture. So guess what? You're much more likely to think to yourself, "Okay, they're serious," and you respect their decision.

When you have bad boundaries, "no" doesn't always mean "no," and the other person gets to recognise that. So what they do then is start pushing the limits when you do say "no" because they've realised that you usually give in anyway. Why should they respect what you're saying this time?

It all sounds so easy, doesn't it? But when you're not used to saying "no," there are all sorts of other feelings that you tend to bring in to weaken your resolve even more.

How many of you can hold your hands up to having done the following:

- Feeling guilty when you said no.
- Rerunning the scene over in your mind and expecting some form of retaliation from the person you said "no" to.
- Finding excuses for not having said "no" that you think are more than enough reason to justify caving in.
- Feeling an ache in the pit of your stomach, a lump in your throat or some other physical manifestation at the thought of having to say "no."
- Starting to feel fear or anxiety about having to say "no."
- Fearing rejection or abandonment if you say "no."

How many of those did you say "yes" to? One? More than one? Hang your head in shame!

Just joking folks!

∞∞∞∞∞∞

So, how are you meant to go about resolving your boundary issues? Well, first of all remember that Rome wasn't built in a day... They had to set up their boundaries first!

This process will take a bit of time. When you're not used to doing something, and it feels so contrary to your nature, you have to start off with baby steps and gradually build yourself up until you have boundaries that you feel comfortable with.

You will probably find that you have to deal with feelings of guilt and anxiety when you first begin to put proper boundaries in place. But once you've tested this a few times, you'll feel much braver about it. Once you realise that the whole world doesn't implode and the person you're setting straight doesn't go completely mental at you, then your confidence will begin to grow and it will all become much easier the next time around!

How to start setting up your boundaries

As we have seen before, boundaries exist to ensure that you're not being denied proper care and consideration from others, and to make sure that you don't forsake yourself. If you want to live a life which offers you satisfaction, you need to have personal guidelines (boundaries) in place for what makes you feel good. So, as we're in the (re)construction business, - imagine you're an architect and rather as you would if you were putting fences up around your garden, decide what form you want your inner landscape (how you feel inside) to take:

- If you'd like more time for yourself, then set up a boundary that will protect your time.
- If you feel that you're doing more than your fair share of the chores, then set a boundary that means that you'll say when you feel you're doing too much.
- If you don't feel that you're getting enough respect, then decide what you need to have in order to feel esteemed - and be ready to explain why you think that you are being devalued.

There are no right or wrong requests. Your boundaries are what you require in order to feel happy, appreciated, respected and cared for. As such, they have as much right to exist as the next person's.

This next list should help you in the boundary building process. As you probably haven't been very good at having boundaries so far in your life, it might be a help to know what you're absolutely entitled to refuse.

Remember, you do have a right to say no to:

- Criticism – You don't deserve it, and no, it's not normal to be criticised on an on-going, regular, unjustified basis.
- Humiliation – You should not be humiliated by anyone, under any circumstances.
- Anger – You do not have to bear the brunt of anyone's anger. You are not someone else's whipping post for their own undigested issues.
- Inconsistency – You have the right to have people treat you with consistency. It's not okay for them to sell you the moon and then disappear... then come back... then be unreliable... *You get my point!*
- Being coerced – You don't have to do something just because everyone is telling you to. Or, you don't have to be harried into making on the spot decisions that make you uncomfortable.
- Unreasonable requests – You can protect your best interests and say no when you don't have time, or don't want to do what is being asked of you, or have other priorities.
- Rejection – You have a right to say what is good for you and to expect that it be taken into account and put in place, without fear of reprisals or abandonment.

Of course, these are just a few examples. There are many, many more!

Setting up your boundaries

Be firm. Be clear. Be considerate.

In other words, when you've established your boundaries it will be because they are right for you, and if they're not taken into consideration you won't feel valued or fulfilled. So state your boundaries clearly when you need to - and **mean** it. As you'll be new to this, you must make sure in the first few weeks that your boundaries are genuine and not coming from a place of unresolved neediness which might make you trample over someone else's personal limits. So think your boundaries through clearly because in order for them to be useful to you, they should be ones that allow you to stay true to yourself.

Explain, but do not feel the need to justify or defend.

Your boundaries are your right as a human being. If you have to explain them to someone then do so distinctly, but without justifying them. You don't have to defend them: they just are!

Do not give in.

This is probably the most difficult part for those of us who don't have good boundaries. We're so used to giving in that standing our ground without feeling that it might turn into a major conflict is going to take a lot of courage. But once you've done it once or twice you'll get used to it, and it'll become less complicated each time. Get yourself some support so that you can get feedback about whether or not you're right to set up this boundary. Sometimes hearing someone else confirm that you're right can be very helpful.

However, don't take it to the other extreme and use it as a way of undermining the other person. You don't want your new-found boundaries to become a battering ram to be used against other people. They're there to keep you secure, but if they're causing distress to anyone else, you might need to check that they haven't turned into barriers. Once you've established them, verify that they're uninfluenced boundaries, and that you haven't altered them through pressure from someone else.

Handling other people's reactions.

If you've set your boundary and made it respectful towards others, then their reactions to it are not your cross to bear. You're only ever responsible for yourself. Other people's behaviour and responses to your boundaries are not your concern... (That takes you back to the good old days, doesn't it?)

∞∞∞∞∞

Once your boundaries are good and are beginning to be established, you should be able to ask yourself the following questions and feel no guilt or panic when you answer yes:

- I have appropriate boundaries and I have the right to ask that they be respected.
- I know that boundaries are my right and having them doesn't make me a selfish person.
- Having boundaries is a sign of self-love, but that doesn't stop me from being loving and kind to others.
- Putting myself first means that I actually now have more to give others and my giving is of better quality because I have boundaries.
- I am not responsible for other people's reactions to my essential boundaries.

How to do it examples

As boundary-setting doesn't need to (and should not) be justified, most of your "action" will come from quietly putting the boundaries into place inside of you and making sure they're respected by those on the outside. It's all in the ***mojo***!

So here are a few examples of how to set up boundaries to get you started:

1. If you believe that your feelings aren't taken into account and this is making you unhappy, then you have to set up a boundary that protects them. You do this by clarifying inside you which feelings are not being respected and then explaining to the other person what is going on for you, and what it is that you require from them.

   Gail felt that Matthew didn't include her in the decision-making for the running of the household and it made her feel as though her opinion didn't count. She explained to him that having him make all the decisions without consulting her made her feel that she wasn't valued and that she didn't have a real place in the house.

   He'd never seen things from this perspective and apologised. Now they set a time for making plans and find solutions that are good for both of them.

   Gail set her boundary, she wanted to feel valued and an equal partner in the household. She explained the reasons for it clearly to Matthew and he was very open to the change.

2. *Michelle was feeling taken for granted and undervalued. Annabel, her teenage daughter, kept giving her lists of demands and Michelle felt that Annabel wasn't giving her due consi-*

deration for all that she already did for her. Michelle told Annabel quite firmly what her limits were.

"I think that you're not taking into account the fact that I work, take care of the home and juggle all the extras. I feel that I don't have enough time for myself and will be putting into place some "me" time in the next few weeks. Although I would love to be able to do what you're asking me to, I feel that this time you should take care of it yourself as it's your responsibility."

Here Michelle handed back responsibility to the person it belonged to: Annabel. Additionally, she was clear about her boundaries and stated what she intended to do. Now she has to stay firm and start giving herself some "me" time. People can't respect your boundaries if you don't respect them yourself!

3. *Louis was not good at saying "no" and frequently felt taken advantage of. His best friend was used to him dropping everything and coming to help her when she asked him to. What he really wanted to do was tell her he couldn't continue to run round every time she had a problem, but it made him feel very guilty.*

The next time she called him to ask him to come over, he had to be clear about what he was prepared to do: "I'd be very happy to help you out, but it's not possible at this moment in time. I suggest coming over on Tuesday when I have more spare time and I can help you then."

He didn't get into a discussion with her and start negotiating. He stopped himself from feeling guilty. He set his limits kindly and respectfully and kept to them.

4. On the spot boundaries:

    - *I don't accept that you keep criticising me and I'm asking you to stop or I shall not continue this discussion. I found what you said just now quite humiliating and I would prefer that you didn't say things like that about me again.*
    - *I'm not willing to stay here whilst you shout at me. Please stop, or I will have to leave the room.*
    - *I find it unsettling when you say that you want to spend time with me but then I don't hear from you for a few days. I would like more consistency between what you say and what you do.*
    - *You're pressuring me to give you an immediate response without giving me time to think it through. I'm not willing to do that and will be taking a couple of hours before getting back to you.*
    - *You've asked me to lend you more money but I feel that I have lent you enough for the time being. I would like to work out when you will be paying me back.*
    - *I would prefer that you didn't stand so close to me, as it's making me uncomfortable.*

Setting boundaries, when done carefully and respectfully, will make you feel amazing. For possibly the first time in your life you'll be taking care of yourself and ensuring that if others don't respect your limits then you'll take a proactive course of action and remove yourself from the negative environment.

Contrary to popular belief, boundaries are not for people who are difficult and inflexible. They're for people who know themselves well and who want to live in harmony with who they are. The first few times that you decide not to cave in when someone starts pushing at one of your boundaries, you're likely to feel guilt, panic or fear. What if they have a really bad reaction to you standing your ground? What if they abandon you because you're not giving way? What if the world starts collapsing? Don't worry, it won't, and you won't either! When you've done it a few times, you'll realise just how simple it is, and you'll be surprised by people's reactions. Most of the time, if they even notice what you're doing (crazy thought!) they'll just tend to tag along with it quite naturally. You'll be amazed by how easy it all is!

Having boundaries is the first element to set up when you want to reclaim your personal power and change your life. It will seem miraculous because you'll feel the effects on you and your life almost immediately.

So put away your well-worn doormat and grab your cement trowel... You've got some boundaries to set up!

Chapter 2

Needs and wants; but not the brattish kind

Needs are those fundamental requirements we all have and keeping them satisfied is absolutely essential to our well-being. They should automatically be fulfilled and are definitely necessary to us, as without having our needs satisfied we cannot be fully content and happy, even though we might be trying really hard to be. Many of us might have lost sight of our needs as we can confuse having them with "wants", which can often be selfish and demanding. Or we might have grown used to ignoring our needs to the point where we become convinced they might all be unreasonable wants that should be dismissed. Or it can also be because those of us who aren't in touch with our needs are very often in contact with people who seem to have no problem in being quite forceful about getting you to meet their supposed needs, so it put us off having our own!

As a result we are even more reticent when it comes to asking for what is good and right for us. We're already not used to it and find it difficult to do, but then we can't help associating asking to have our needs met with being demanding and unreasonable. After all, that's often what the other person has shown us through their behaviour when they're asking for their "needs" to be met, and who wants to be like them?

Applying the "selfish" label is another means we can use to let ourselves off the hook for not listening to our needs and giving ourselves what we require. Saying that we don't want to be selfish (as it would take time and care away from others if we looked after ourselves) helps us to bury the guilt we should feel about letting ourselves down so badly. It's often much easier to stay in "victim mode" rather than to shake ourselves up and be proactive about giving to ourselves. ***Harsh to hear; but true.***

Again, a lot of this starts in our childhood, when our parents (or other significant adults) showed us by their behaviour towards us that expressing our needs was not permissible, and from then on our needs were probably routinely not taken into account. You might have met a fair bit of judgement when you were expressing your needs and could even have got a label or two handed out and stuck on your forehead! You become known as that needy, or capricious, or difficult person... As a result of this, and possibly to avoid the uncomfortable feeling you get from the tags you've been attributed, you accept having your needs discounted, and you even start doing it to yourself.

However, this isn't the case for everyone. Having your needs whittled away does not necessarily start in childhood and can come later in life through different experiences you may have. It can occur through another person's influence or maybe from events over which you had very little control and which slowly eroded your confidence in your needs until you tolerate the fact that they are no longer validated. Or you might subconsciously have chosen to give them up yourself as you tried to make a relationship work: trying too hard to please or make the other person happy may have lured you into giving up your rights to your needs.

How many of you can hold your hands up to having, at some stage in your life, told yourself things like, "It doesn't matter, you can always do it another day," or "Let them have it, you don't really need it anyway," or "They might think you're being selfish if you say you need to have some time alone, or more nurture, or kindness…"

Fill in your own blank.

How did it really make you feel afterwards when you had yet again discounted your needs? Bloomin' marvellous, I'm sure!

The other way that you can start to ignore your needs (and which many of us don't even think of) is by living with a parent or other adult who is also in denial of their needs. You inevitably copy what you see and also put up with not having your feelings and needs taken care of.

For instance, here's a classic case: what about when your mother asks that everyone take their shoes off when they come home because she's spent all day cleaning and needs to feel that she's appreciated by having you respect her hard work? If no one pays any attention to her (no boundaries) and she has to start over and does so without really saying anything (out of touch with her feelings), then you know you're watching someone who's also neglecting her needs. This kind of scene doesn't happen in a family where the adults are showing the children that needs are to be valued. Everyone would be too respectful of each other to just walk in and dirty the house immediately.

The more we give up on our needs, the less we are even conscious of the process and it sadly becomes perfectly normal to disregard our needs and stand by whilst others also do it. We kid ourselves into accepting it as standard practice and we begin to believe that's what life is all about.

∞∞∞∞∞

Needs versus Wants

So what's a guy or gal to do when they're not used to recognising their needs, and how do you know if they're legit?

Needs are those things which are essential to you in order to make you feel great!

They are what you *need* (☺) as much of as possible so you can take your levels of satisfaction, fulfilment and just plain *joie de vivre* to 100%.

But just so we're clear here, when you're not feeling great most of the time, and haven't been for a while, you might either be completely ignoring your needs, or you might have started mixing up what is actually indispensable to you with things that seem very important right now but aren't necessarily. What happens then is that you can develop what feels like strong needs, but which in actual fact are just coping mechanisms to fill your inner void. Your real needs have become distorted and have turned into needy wants; they're not the same thing at all.

Wants are not essential. We may want more ice cream, but we don't actually need it! We can confuse wants as needs when we are living a life of inner poverty. Wants begin to take up more room and become more important than they should because you are not being fulfilled on a more fundamental level.

Do you know what I mean? Wants can become extreme. You might be someone who is constantly asking for attention, or who appears to be permanently unsatisfied. Or what about those people who seem to be continually asking for more? Or again, those who are very often in a bad mood, or angry? You can't help but look at them and wonder what their problem is and why they're so demanding. Well, usually it's because they're psychologically unhealthy through not meeting their own needs, and so they may progressively try to feel they "exist" and be validated by others through their increasingly erratic and imposing demands.

Below are some examples which will help you to understand the impact which not honouring your real needs can have on your state of mind, and consequently on your relationships:

Bill was finding Hector increasingly bullying. When Bill told him that he wanted to go out to the cinema with him on Friday, Hector started calling Bill selfish and said he wasn't thinking about him and how tired he was. He said that what he really wanted was to stay in and relax and went on and on about it until Bill finally caved in.

The problem here isn't that Hector was tired, or that Bill was being selfish. What was going on in this scenario was that Hector had not been taking good care (legitimate need) of himself, and had been overworking. As Hector was not used to taking good care of this particular need, instead of recognising that this was the issue, he interpreted what was going on for him as him needing (whiney want) to have more time to relax. What he really needed in order to feel better was to slow down his pace at work and give himself more consideration on a regular basis to keep up his feel-good levels.

Martha was becoming angry with Theo because he just didn't seem to get the fact that she felt she was doing more than her share of the household chores. The resentment was building and in her head she was becoming more insistent that what she really wanted was some time apart in order to think about their relationship. She was also making sure that Theo knew damn well what she thought about his behaviour.

The problem wasn't so much Theo's behaviour but Martha's reaction to this set of circumstances in her life. As she was not recognising her real needs, which were for kindness and support (legitimate need), she had gone off into outrage and had translated that as meaning that her relationship was no longer working and thinking she wanted (whiney want) time out. If she had been fulfilling her primary needs, then her feelings about her relationship would not have built up the way they had.

Do you see how not protecting your needs can have an impact in insidious ways? So much gets twisted when you're reducing yourself and not giving yourself what you need. Circumstances that could be handled another way and which would affect you differently can get distorted and start creating an even bigger crisis. Having legitimate needs and respecting them makes for more stability in your life, meaning events appear less complicated, so you can concentrate more on the good times.

When you start asking yourself what your needs really are, you'll want to be sure that you come from a place where it's not the impoverished, uncared-for part of you that speaks up. You want to be clear that it's the real you that you're hearing so that you can start to put in place boundaries that will preserve those genuine needs.

We all have needs. It's just that some of us have forgotten that they serve a purpose and are our due. So hands up who wants them back, and *now!*

∞∞∞∞∞

What are legitimate needs?

I think by now you'll have gathered that it's normal to have needs and absolutely not natural to think you have none, or to ignore them. Sorting through what are legitimate needs and what might be needy ego helps establish healthy "wants."

Some of you might have forgotten what needs even mean, or

it might be vague at best, so below are examples of categories of legitimate needs that should be met:

1. **Emotional needs:** love, respect, care, empathy, kindness, validation, nurture, support, compassion, generosity, acceptance, belonging, happiness, serenity.
2. **Intellectual needs:** self-expression, unrestricted thoughts and ideas, challenges, knowledge, stimulation, imagination, creativity, encouragement, self-development.
3. **Personal needs:** growth as a person, being authentic, living in congruence with your ideology, acceptance, confidence, self-esteem.
4. **Social needs:** friends and family, interaction, cooperation, inclusion, belonging, relaxation, activities, fulfilling employment.
5. **Material needs:** clothing, shelter, food and water, warmth, exercise, safety, sleep, health.

These are all cases of legitimate needs. As we saw earlier on in this chapter, without them, you'll find it difficult to live a life in which you're satisfied and joyful. Unfortunately, when you've grown used to ignoring some or all or your needs, or having them dismissed by other people, you might no longer know what they are and can make the mistake of rejecting them when they try to make themselves heard.

Or you might have developed what you think are a set of needs but which are actually intense wants. The examples above will help you to start sorting through them so that you can either discard them or find the legitimate needs hiding behind them.

As an example, when you mistake your legitimate needs for whiney wants you might become guilty of overruling them, which will have a knock-on effect on your self-esteem (see how this all links together?). Self-esteem cannot flourish when you're denying fundamental parts of yourself, which of course you would be doing if you reject your needs. When you have low self-esteem, you'll never be able to feel on top of the world, no matter what. Are you beginning to understand the importance of not neglecting your needs? Like your boundaries, they're crucial for your well-being.

∞∞∞∞∞

So many of us make the mistake of thinking that we're not directly responsible for getting our needs met. We tend to think that it's up to others to respect our needs and fill them for us. But that doesn't ever work, and for the following reason:

> *If you have a hard time knowing what it is you really need, then how on earth can you logically expect someone else to know?*

Only we can be in charge of getting our needs met. If you carry on saying what it is that the other person is not giving to you and holding them accountable for not meeting your needs then chances are that, in 50 years, you'll still be waiting. You alone can decide what is missing in your life that you genuinely need to have. Then you have to put yourself in charge of validating those needs, explaining kindly to others why you want them respected, and making sure that you enrich your life by giving your needs as much consideration as possible.

When we are used to expecting others to fulfil our needs, it unfortunately doesn't take long before we can start blaming them when we feel that they are not being met. This obviously doesn't make for happy relationships, or for creating internal contentment. The following examples will show you how having a need that is not expressed, and which is therefore not being met, can be turned into judgement and blame:

> *Harry had been feeling low and all he wanted was for Catherine to see this and to give him a bit of extra care and attention. Catherine had been really busy all day and was still rushing around in the evening making dinner and seeing to the children's homework at the same time. When Harry came back from the office, she didn't come and say hello to him as she usually did and so he felt even more let down.*

Instead of being able to say what was really going on for him, he turned on Catherine and started criticising the fact that there was too much noise and bustle in the kitchen.

Or:

> *Maria had been feeling unloved, but she wasn't used to pinpointing her needs and didn't know how to name them. She started to blame Hal for this feeling by telling him that he was spending too much time at work and that he obviously loved his job more than he loved her.*

Her need for closeness was not being met, but she was only able to voice it in a negative way which Hal couldn't hear because he was feeling attacked.

Or:

> *Jo was feeling insecure because she had had a bad day at the office and her boss was really on her case. She was looking forward to going home because she wanted Mike to make her feel better. However, when she did get home, he had left a note saying he had forgotten he was meeting up with a friend and he would be back later than usual.*
>
> *When he did get back, Jo told him that he was selfish and that she couldn't rely on him. She gave him examples of things she*

had asked him to do that he hadn't. Mike was understandably not impressed and told her that she was being totally unreasonable.

What was going on here was that Jo's need for reassurance and support had not been met and when Mike wasn't there to give it to her, it made her feel even worse, so she overreacted. If she had recognised her need, she wouldn't have minded having to wait until he got back in order to ask for what she needed.

As you've probably realised from the examples above, one of the main problems of not having your needs met is that you tend to voice it in a way that could be aggressive or critical. This means that the other person is less likely to really "hear" what it is you are trying to say. As you know from when this happens to you, we go straight into defence mode when we're feeling attacked, and so the message gets lost.

We are really able to build a different world for our Self when we can clearly state what it is that we need, rather than trying to get it fulfilled through saying what's wrong with the other person or their behaviour. Perhaps, if your needs were being met more regularly, you might not actually have gotten to the stage where you thought there was something wrong with the other person's behaviour. You wouldn't be suffering from lack of nurture and your relationship would be much healthier as a result.

However, being invited to say what it is that we need is a question that we've probably never been asked before, and it's unlikely that we've stopped to ask it of ourselves either. All we tend to sense are the feelings that rise up when our needs aren't being met… You know, those moments when you feel rejected, hurt or angry because you've done something kind, loving, or just plain normal, but it always seems to be a one way street and you never appear to get your needs met...

∞∞∞∞∞

Finding your needs

"Okay, I'm sure you're probably wondering when I'm going to get around to helping you sort out your real needs from your whiney wants. So I'll respect your *needs* and give you what you *want!*" *(*Sorry, couldn't help the corny joke*)*.

Here's a really good technique for trying to sort out your needs for those of you who are so unused to knowing what they are:

> *Keep asking yourself what you really need, and don't give up until you finally realise there is an answer, no matter how hidden.*

What? You're saying that's impossible? If your needs have been that buried for that long, you can keep asking yourself until you're blue in the face and strictly nothing seems to come out. Man, you're a tough nut to crack, aren't you?

Okay then, here's a really easy way to do it... of course I was going to try to get you to do it the hard way first! How else were you going to realise that you really had no idea what your real needs were? ☺

> The next time you feel great, or happy, or powerful and you seem to just be surfing along on the crest of life, actually ask yourself what's going on that's contributing to all these really positive feelings that you're having. You'll soon realise why it is that you're feeling just so amazing, and that will then become your first recognised need. You now know that you *need* some of this in

order to give you this incredible state of mind.

For instance:

> *Simon had been feeling pretty morose for a few days before the weekend, when he'd planned to go wind surfing. When he was out there on the water, the negative thoughts about his week fell away and he began to feel on top of the world. He laughed when it suddenly struck him that the reason that he felt so wonderful wasn't because he was out in the open air racing along, although that certainly played a huge part. It was actually because he had taken time out to do some well-needed exercise and he felt overjoyed to have given himself this gift.*

So you see, the need that was to be recognised here wasn't the one he would have thought it was, like feeling powerful and in charge on the wind surfer, but the much deeper need of being kind and giving himself some essential care.

> *Carol was feeling exhausted after coming back from her trip but couldn't understand why, because she had mixed business with pleasure and had actually had a fantastic time during the past five days. She'd given a presentation that had been well received by her clients and had even been able to snatch a few hours to walk around and see the sights.*

> *As the plane landed, she suddenly understood why her mood had been dampened. It was because she was going to have to go back to work where her boss was too demanding and not appreciative of all that she did. She realised that she had enjoyed the intellectual challenge that the presentation had given her because it made her feel exhilarated when she had pulled it all together.*

Carol realised that her work environment wasn't exciting and was not making her happy. She recognised her need for stimulation and acknowledgement and knew she would have to start looking for a job that fulfilled these needs.

To help you start identifying some of your needs, think of a recent moment where you have felt your best. If one doesn't spring to mind, then think back to some occasions in the past that really stand out for you and ask yourself what needs were being met at that time. Very soon, you'll start to see a pattern emerging and you'll begin to discern which needs are necessary for your well-being.

You can refer back to the list on Page 41 for examples of needs, though of course there are many more than the ones I've listed. Now that you've got the ball rolling, I'm sure that you can think of plenty of great needs of your own. If chocolate comes up as a need, though, then you know you haven't quite got the hang of it yet!

Meeting your needs

As we saw earlier, it's not up to someone else to give you what you need: that's not their role. So if you're not getting what you need, there's no point trying to turn around and point the finger of blame at anyone else. Unfortunately, as you're beginning to find out, you only have yourself to "blame", which is great actually because it means that you're becoming more aware of why you weren't doing so well and with it comes the novel idea that **you** can do something about it. It's no longer a case of put up, and shut up. You've got all the power you want to give yourself to change the situation.

You're in charge, you're the leader!

Now that you're beginning to discover your needs and are realising that you're responsible for fulfilling them, it's also time to let other people know what they are. After all, possibly for many years your needs have been ignored and now you're going to reintroduce them. It's only fair to make the other people in your life aware of your new-found needs, but we have to be attentive to others and to how we put across the information. As we saw earlier, when we make our needs known through attack or blame, other people quite rightly can't hear you. So here's where we look at how to be able to say what your needs are, now that you are beginning to know for yourself!

Learning to ask for what you need

As stated above, once you've started to establish your list of needs, chances are that not many people in your entourage will know what they are, since you've been keeping them nice and secret! You'll have to explain what your needs are, and why you're requesting that they be respected.

We would only want to acknowledge other people's needs in a positive and empathetic way, and the same goes for them; we wouldn't want anyone to respond to our needs out of guilt, shame or fear. Being careful about how you communicate your needs is not just about making sure that people can hear you. It's also about being confident that they'll be willing to help you fulfil your needs because they're not at their expense.

Look at it this way: it's like sharing a duvet. If the other person is used to having most of it and you try and grab some back, chances are you're in for a tug of war. If however, you tell them that you've been feeling the cold more and could do with sharing more of the covers, they're not going to turn you down are they? They'll just snuggle up closer if you convey your message properly. It's all in the presentation!

Below you'll find the simple process I used when I first started establishing my needs. It really helped me in defining them for other people to understand so that they would be able to accept and integrate them into our relationship.

1. **Step 1:** Establish what your need is by using the method about finding your needs which starts on page 45.
2. **Step 2:** Explain to the other person what this need is and where it comes from. Clarify the reasoning behind it and what your experience of it is.
3. **Step 3:** If you can, say what your feelings are (this is

good general practice for being as much in touch with yourself as possible. But please don't worry if you don't get anything at this stage).

4. **Step 4:** Make your need inclusive of the other person so that they don't feel threatened or pressured by your "need".

NB: I feel that it's really important at this point to emphasise that your needs and feelings are yours and no-one else's. We don't all feel the same way about the various events and people that we encounter. Feelings are subjective, so you must own them: "I felt hurt" and not "You made me feel hurt". If you slip into blame mode when sharing your feelings or needs, then you're not taking ownership of them. If you don't "own" them, you're not in control of your own power and that's not a place you want to be anymore, right?

Here are some examples of how to put your message across in a non-antagonistic way. You're much more likely to get a positive response and to see movement when you're able to say what it is that you need in a manner that is clear and calm.

Alice had understood that her need for intellectual stimulation was very important. She'd wanted to continue her studies for a while, but had kept putting it off as she thought the time away from her family wasn't workable. On the few occasions when she had tried to talk to Tom about it, he had just nodded and not taken the conversation any further. Now that she recognised her need and realised that she had been procrastinating because of her lack of self-esteem, Alice decided to bring the subject up again.

Step 1: *Alice recognised her need for intellectual stimulation.*

Step 2: *She asked Tom when it would be a good time for her to talk to him and have his full attention. During the ensuing conversation, she made it clear to Tom that she needed intellectual stimulation in order to feel fulfilled and happy. She explained that this need was not being fulfilled and that it was important to her that this part of her be acknowledged.*

Step 3: (Don't forget at this point what I mentioned about feelings and needs earlier on. They're yours to acknowledge and yours to own.)

Alice explained that she had felt hurt when she had tried to broach the subject before because she felt that he hadn't listened to her properly. She had since realised that she hadn't emphasised how important this subject was to her. She made this clear to Tom who straight away stopped what he was doing and paid attention.

Step 4: *Alice said that she would like to attend the school she had found, starting in September, and told Tom that she could only put this project into motion with his help. She would appreciate his ideas on what new arrangements would have to be put into place.*

By being clear about what she needed and why, Alice was allowing Tom to have a full understanding of her reasons for wanting to go back to school. In explaining it to him, Alice was assertive about what she needed and kept her language positive. She was able to get her need across in a way that Tom could hear and accept.

Deborah felt that her need for respect and support was not being met by her partner Geoffrey. He would invariably come home from work and complain about the day he'd just had. When she tried to voice her feelings about her day, he seemed to dismiss what she said and she interpreted this as though he didn't care and thought her job wasn't as important as his.

Step 1: *Deborah recognised her need for respect and support.*

Step 2: *She told Geoffrey that she would appreciate having a discussion with him as she felt that her needs for help and validation were not being met.*

Step 3: *She explained that she realised she needed his undivided attention when she was trying to say how her day had been, otherwise she didn't feel appreciated. This made her feel that he didn't value her contributions to their relationship, and that made her feel frustrated and angry.*

Step 4: *Deborah asked Geoffrey if they could take it in turns to listen to each other at the end of the day and give each other mutual support and attention.*

In this way Deborah was able to voice her dissatisfaction in a reasoned and precise manner. She didn't make Geoffrey feel that he was being blamed for anything and she put forward a solution which would work for both of them.

As with your boundaries, you don't need to be apologetic about what your needs are; nor your desire to have them met. If you're specific about your needs and are able to convey clearly the manner in which the situation affects you, it'll help other people be able to understand and accept your request. Being assertive not only does wonders for your self-esteem, it also makes the other person less inclined to dismiss what you're saying. I can't tell you how free you begin to feel when you start being assertive; it's amazing!

As you get used to asking for what you need, the shadow of guilt that might have hung around when you tried to do it in the past will disappear. The more you do it, the more you'll realise that getting your needs met is legitimate and fair.

How to do it examples

Needs are not just about satisfying the fundamental requirements we have in order to lead a healthy and contented life. They're about a state of being with regards to our Self; one in which we confidently put ourselves first, in the heartfelt knowledge of our true worth. We reach a stage where we **want** to give to ourselves because we love who we are. (The whole concept of loving yourself might feel strange, or for some, extremely far-fetched at this point. But believe me, it will come and you'll be left wondering how you managed before. Please look forward to it!)

There's one very important condition to achieving this state of being and it's probably the one we overlook the most frequently. For me, this aspect is the absolute prerequisite for general well-being and happiness: *we have to maintain a comfortable level of care and nurture towards ourselves on a daily basis.* A little bit of self-love can go a long way, and we should keep up an awareness of giving to ourselves very regularly.

Each day, ask yourself just this one question: "What can I do for myself today to give me a dose of well-deserved loving attention?" Below is a little list of questions that you can ask yourself to help you discover ways to give yourself some ongoing TLC.

- **What do you enjoy doing?** When you establish this, make sure those things are top of your list of to do's, at

least once a week.
- **Who are the people who make you feel valued?** Find time to see them or phone them as often as you can. Make seeing them a priority as they make you feel great and that's what you need in your life.
- **What activities do you really enjoy?** Going to a restaurant, the cinema, the theatre? Make sure you program these kinds of treats into your diary.
- **Which places do I feel good?** Make sure you get to go there regularly.
- **What kind of physical activity gives you a buzz?** Build that power walk with your friend into your weekly routine. Go to the gym and make it a priority. Take a stroll through the park. You get an automatic lift from getting physical (in any way possible!), so even if your heart initially sinks at the thought, find something that you like to do and do it regularly. You'll feel the difference immediately.

And on a more modest (and even more accessible) scale:

- Have that warm bath you keep telling yourself you don't have time for. Get out the candles, the flowers and the wine.
- Read that book curled up on the sofa for 30 minutes or more. **Nothing** is going to fall apart that quickly if you take some time out!
- Treat yourself to something new, or a pampering session at the spa, or that haircut you've been promising yourself.
- Dance and sing wildly at home because you want to.
- Go to bed early if that's what you're craving.

You get the idea...

You don't and shouldn't need any reasons for showing some kindness to yourself, because as a well-known beauty company is always telling you: *YOU'RE WORTH IT*!

As we've just seen, having needs and honouring them are a vital part of feeling complete and satisfied. When your needs are fulfilled, you're more likely to feel content and balanced as a person. You'll no longer feel desolate because that void in you keeps growing, or be subject to having wild wants that might have grown to exist only because the inner you was being deprived of care and nurture. We can never be psychologically healthy or thriving when we're negating our needs; they are absolutely essential to our well-being.

Now you've got your head around the first two chapters, but there are still three to come. I hope however that you'll be eager to crack on; as I'm sure you're beginning to experience the difference for yourself just with the few changes you might already have made. Feeling good makes you want to keep going, doesn't it?

We're going to move on now to meet another whole set of elements without which you'll find it complicated to be a fully flourishing person. I know it sounds tough, and some of you might think that your lives are already quite good, thank you very much; but if you're not also in touch with your feelings then you'll not get to those heady heights of personal satisfaction and contentment that you can achieve. So, deep breath here, and *"courage mon brave!"* as they say in France.

Chapter 3

Feelings; but without the pain

Feelings fill our senses and make us feel alive. Without them it's impossible to be entirely serene and happy and we can become very empty people indeed. It's our feelings that give life meaning and, as such, our aim should be to have as many positive feelings in our life as possible. The fact of supressing our feelings means that our behaviour and reactions will be tainted by the emptiness that has been created inside us. We can't help but have unreliable reactions to things when we haven't got the rock-solid base of security which comes from being in touch with our feelings.

Feelings are felt throughout our body: when we feel good, our whole body feels alive, vibrant and healthy. When we feel down, our body is also a reflection of that. And, in the long term, living in denial of our feelings can actually lead to disease.

Do you remember how it felt when you were young? Everything seemed to be in multicolour; all your feelings and emotions were experienced with a buoyancy and strength that you may have lost sight of as you became an adult. Through negating your feelings or dumbing them down, not only do you reduce yourself, but you also diminish your capacity to sense the world in the same intense way. You know how it is, you get told "don't cry" or "it didn't really hurt" or "get over it" etc. until the training to ignore your feelings is well under way.

Unfortunately, through negating your feelings, the ones which you probably sense the most frequently are the negative ones: pain, distress, depression, apathy, hopelessness. I'm not deliberately painting a negative picture, but those of us who realise how far removed we are from our feelings will probably be able to nod their heads at this stage as they realise that this does indeed seem to be the case. More importantly, as we diminish how much we can feel in order to avoid these uncomfortable sensations, it can also have a knock-on effect on how we sense the more positive feelings, and we may wind up in a constant grey zone with very little to uplift us or give us enjoyment.

∞∞∞∞∞

What are feelings?

I think it's appropriate at this stage to have another dictionary definition, this time for feelings. It's useful to do this because this way you'll be even more aware of what you might be missing out on! We all talk about our feelings and say we're feeling this and that, but often we're just in contact with the four main groups of feelings, which are mad, glad, sad or fear. All the subtler variations are not often felt by the majority of us, but it's those emotions that we should really be in contact with as they give us our passion and vitality.

When we connect with mad, glad, sad or fear, it's usually because they're such strong feelings that we can't bury or ignore them. It's a shame, and it's exhausting that often we can only heed the warnings that our feelings are trying to give us when they hit us full on through the guise of mad, sad or fear. Being in touch with the subtler feelings would allow us to hear them so much earlier before the experience we were confronting had taken its toll on us.

Many of you might find it difficult to describe your finer feelings, and it's the same old story as in the previous two chapters: if there are bits of you that you can't reach, then you can't thrive. Being in touch with your subtler feelings refreshes the parts that otherwise lie forgotten. After all, these feelings are there to act as a clear signal to you that you don't feel comfortable or happy right now and need to attend to what's going on. Or conversely, that you're feeling great, in which case you need to concentrate and make sure that you keep giving yourself more of the same. Feelings keep you on track about what you need to feel fulfilled and flourishing. When you get used to having them ignored by others or by yourself, then you're giving yourself an invitation to live a life which won't be able to offer you full satisfaction or joy, or at best only fleetingly.

Being aware of your feelings is also a way of sorting through some of the rubbish that comes flying at you at different moments of your life. When you're really in touch with how you feel about something, it means you can deal with it as it happens and recover from it, instead of concealing it inside you and dragging its rotting carcass with you as you go. Gross!

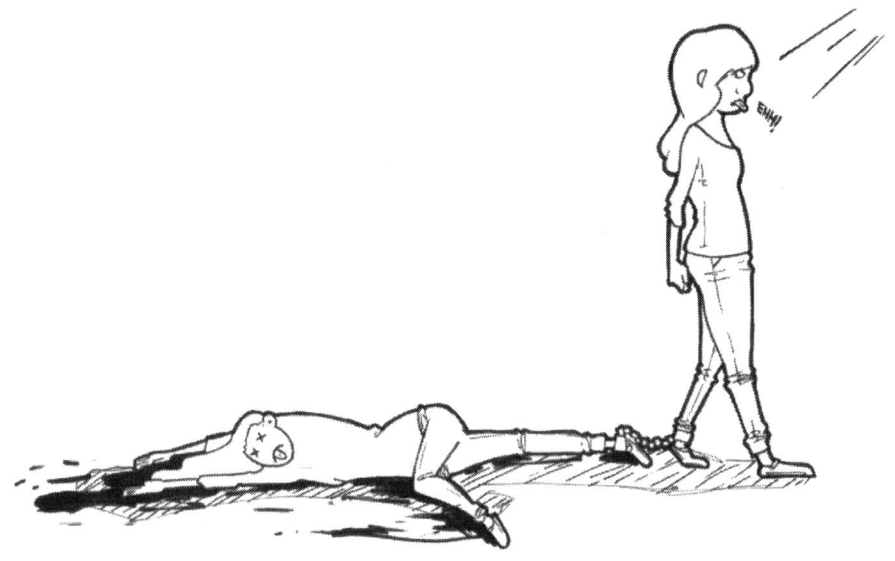

So, back to the definition of feelings – thought you'd got away without it, didn't you? As with the other definition for boundaries which I gave earlier, having a clear one for feelings will really help you to get your head around what they represent. This'll be useful when you begin to voluntarily track them.

Feelings are:

- A physical sensation that arises in you through fear, warmth, pain etc.
- A state of consciousness (being) that is experienced through emotions, thoughts and desires.

The first definition will be very useful to us later on in this chapter when we see how we can use our bodily sensations as a way of recognising that our feelings are trying to talk to us. The second one pretty much sums up everything to do with the kind of fluid, internal feelings we've been talking about up until this point. Feelings occur naturally because of your emotional response to events, **but** they also exist because of what you think and what you believe you want.

Okay, deep breath here, 'cos the going will be a bit tough for the next few minutes!

"Feelings are attributed to a human, subjective response." This means that, like it or not, you're responsible for your feelings and what they are. ***Ouch, that hurt!***

That was one really big piece of information in a very short space of time, so I think it's only fair to break it down and make it more user friendly. Don't want you going AWOL on me! Okay, let's take this one step at a time:

1. When you're used to recognising your feelings then, as I said before, you can use them as alarm bells. When the

feelings are negative, you know that you have to do something about the situation you're in. When the feelings are positive, you should look around you and see why you're feeling so good and keep creating events that keep up your feel-good quotas (the more the merrier for this one!).

2. Just as you did with your needs, when you've lost touch with or ignored your feelings they can become distorted and might only really be sensed when they're very strong and you already feel really bad. Had you known how, you would probably have preferred to deal with your circumstances when the subtler feelings came in to play. As you didn't, you may have subconsciously compensated for the ever growing bad sensations you were having by developing intense needs or having very acute (usually) negative feelings. Feeling bogged down by all the information yet?

In other words:

a) You can begin to have distinct desires for things, or very strong needs for things, that you're now convinced are essential to you. This can take the form of developing needy, demanding, or unreasonable behaviour. Or you could deal with it in other ways by developing an eating disorder, drinking too much, cutting yourself off from others etc. These are strategies that you can use as a lever to fill the emotional void inside you. This mutation only comes about because you were no longer really genuinely in touch with your finer feelings.

b) Also, because you're not connected to your feelings you can go from one extreme to another: from having little or no feelings to having a strong outburst of feeling. You can start having intense and unwarranted reactions to situations which surprise not only the people involved, but also yourself rather like a pressure cooker that you forgot on the stove.

Right, here are a few examples to help you understand better, because that was a lot of information to try and assimilate in one go. The examples below will show you how being unable to hear your subtler feelings can create bigger problems for you without your being aware of it:

Andrew was used to ignoring his feelings of insecurity. He had parents who were always asking him, "Are you a man, or a mouse?" and as he grew up, he knew that he had to override these feelings of vulnerability and stick with what was expected of him by being very masculine. As a result, he grew used to ignoring many other subtle feelings, such as being easily flustered, feeling nervous and being apprehensive. The only feeling which really helped him cover up these others (which were too painful for him) was anger, which seemed to arise in him apparently quite unbidden and fairly frequently.

Andrew had lost touch with his finer feelings and he wasn't able to hear their warning about his discomfort so that he could do something about it immediately. This would feed his unacknowledged, more delicate feeling of being vulnerable, and it would grow inside him. As he didn't deal with his feelings when they were still small enough, over time, he would go straight to "mad" and then wonder why he was angry.

Celia was known for being a shopaholic. She couldn't control her desire for new clothes and was constantly hitting the shops and spending lots of money. When she was shopping she felt sexy and beautiful. Whenever she needed cheering up, she would go shopping for the immediate buzz it gave her.

What Celia was covering up when she went on a shopping spree was her negative feelings of not feeling loved and secure. Purchasing new clothes made her feel fantastic, so she didn't have to think about those empty feelings which arose inside her of not being worthy of love. The additional knock-on effect was that it also stopped her from feeling how depressed she was. In this way she was able to ignore how she truly felt and did not do anything about it.

Kate had an overwhelming need to get approval. This desire meant that she quite frequently bulldozed other people and their feelings in order to make herself the centre of attention.

What Kate was really dealing with were her much subtler feelings of insecurity and helplessness. Getting attention was her way of dealing with the emptiness she felt inside. When she was getting praise and recognition it made her feel special, and masked the more painful feelings she was carrying inside her. Not dealing with her subtler feelings meant however that she was damaging her relationships with others which would eventually mean she might have to deal with additional feelings of confusion and loneliness as people began to distance themselves from her.

3. I think the first two points were easy to absorb once I'd clarified them a little, but what I'm going to say next might seem a very hard to believe: when we get used to discerning our range of subtler feelings we'll also begin to realise that we can influence them and even **change them** to positive ones if that's what we decide to do... slaves to our feelings no longer!

I heard your jaw drop when you read that! It is such a big lump to swallow that I can't expect you to do it so quickly, and we'll look at that in more depth a bit later on in this chapter. Until then, tuck the idea away safely in some corner of your brain and let it mature.

∞∞∞∞∞∞

As we saw previously, the broader categories are mad, glad, sad and fear. Within these, we have a whole profusion of subtler emotions. For the more sceptical among you I've included some examples for your delectation!

Mad
Aggressive – anger – belligerent – bitter – complaining – critical – cruel – defensive – disgust – dislike – envy – exasperated – fighting – flustered – frustrated – grumpy – hostile – impatient – indignant – irritated – jealous – manipulative – mean – opinionated – outraged – rage – resentful – scorn – selfish – spiteful – stubborn – sullen – vengeful – vexed – vindictive – violent – wounded

Glad

Admired – adored – aglow – attractive – blissful – bright – calm – caring – cheerful – cherished – compassionate – confident – contented – courageous – eager – elated – energetic – enthusiastic – excited – free – friendly – gentle – glowing – gregarious – happy – hopeful – inspired – joyful – kindly – loving – loyal – optimistic – passionate – peaceful – powerful – relaxed – safe – satisfied – serene – strong – sympathetic – thrilled – trusting – understanding – warm – wonderful

Sad

Abandoned – abused – alone – ashamed – awful – belittled – bored – controlled – crushed – defeated – degraded – demoralised – depressed – desolate – despair – devastated – disappointed – discontented – discouraged – distressed – empty – exploited – forlorn – gloomy – grief – guilt – helpless – hopeless – humiliated – hurt – inadequate – incompetent – inferior – insecure – miserable – mistreated – pessimistic – rejected – shamed – upset – useless – withdrawn – worthless

Fear

Afraid – alarmed – anxious – apprehensive – baffled – cautious – confused – defensive – desperate – distressed – disturbed – fearful – flustered – frightened – intimidated – lost – mistrustful – nervous – overwhelmed – panicky – perplexed – scared – shocked – tense – terrified – threatened – trapped – troubled – uneasy – worried

Bet you didn't know there might be so many, right? That's nothing compared to how many are actually out there waiting for you to discover them. Were you able to pinpoint any of these subtler feelings before? If not, did you find the list helpful?

The more you're able to recognise your feelings and differentiate between them, the greater will be your capacity for reconnecting with yourself. This is when you can look at the list and start deliberately choosing to get as many of the positive (glad) feelings in your life as possible; and of course, deciding which ones of all those negatives you are going to evict from inside you!

Before going any further, here would be a good time to remind you of the inter-relatedness of all of these techniques: as you establish good boundaries and fulfil your needs, you'll find that the frequency of your positive feelings will rise. This is inevitable thankfully. You'll automatically take note of your feelings now that you know why they exist and will begin to endorse them as though it had always been second nature. With this comes even greater news: you'll have realised by now that by changing how you feel about yourself, your view of the world and what it brings you alters, too. You might already be finding this is the case and that you've started to feel much more hopeful and confident. Your happiness levels could even be rising, too!

∞∞∞∞∞

Are you in touch with your feelings?

One of the first ways to check this, of course, is by noting if you could relate to many of the finer feelings that I gave in the previous list. If you could, then evidently you're fairly well in touch with your feelings, but for the majority of us this isn't the case. If you're still not clear where you stand on this one, below is a list of questions that should help you to be really sure:

- I can't answer immediately, if at all, when I'm asked how I feel about something.
- My feelings vocabulary is limited to "fine," as I brush aside my real feelings.
- I lie about my real feelings out of guilt, fear, or another negative reason.
- I put others before me, which means that I am probably invalidating my own feelings.
- I feel resentful of other people's needs and desires.
- I don't dare ask for my feelings to be respected.
- I think I have to justify my feelings.
- I accept having to do things even when I don't want to.
- I can have extreme reactions which aren't necessarily appropriate to the situation.
- I wait for others to take care of my feelings.

If you were nodding your head to some of those then it does mean that you're probably not that much in touch with your feelings and there's still some work to be done. But don't feel bad about it, life is a learning curve and you're doing just fine.

Not respecting your feelings and being used to having them negated by others or invalidated by you means that you're not in harmony with yourself; but you already know that or you wouldn't be reading this book. I imagine that you have been looking for the inner peace which we all wish for. It will be yours if you get in touch with your feelings and give them the due care and attention that they deserve and need. So obviously what you need for me to do now is to give you advice on how to reconnect with those feelings...

How to be in touch with your feelings

Now that you're beginning to get an understanding of how to be in touch with your needs, it'll be easier for you to start the process of connecting with your feelings. With your needs, I suggested that you just maintain an awareness of when you felt particularly fantastic, as that was a clear signal that they were being met. In the same way, you want to make sure that when you're feeling on top of the world, you concentrate on what's going on for you and start asking yourself what finer feelings are also involved.

Unfortunately, it's probably easier to ask you to try to appreciate and describe your finer feelings by starting with a negative scenario. Somehow, we're more likely to find the words to express how we're really feeling when it's an unfavourable situation. You know how it is, you're more likely to notice when you're in a bad mood, or very upset, than you are to take note and say "Hey, I'm feeling great today!" We take it for granted when it's positive. For instance, when faced with a distressing situation, you'll probably be able to come up with a couple of finer feelings that are in relation to it. But when you feel good, you feel good, simple as that!

Here are some case studies to illustrate what can happen when we aren't able pinpoint and respond to our finer feelings:

> *Sam was feeling particularly angry. He'd had a pretty bad day at the office and was raging as he took the tube in the evening. Internally, he was swearing at all the bumbling idiots on their way home, then at the tube driver for pulling in too slowly, then at all the hot steamy armpits in the train. By the time he got home he'd worked himself into a total fury.*
>
> *If you'd asked him how he felt, he would have told you that he was really mad. However, if he'd been able to discern his sub-*

tler feelings, he would've been able to recognise the signs of his growing irritation when his boss made a derogatory comment about his proposal. Instead of sensing his feelings of inadequacy and of being demoralised, he missed them entirely and it all snowballed from there.

What Sam could have done, if he had only known, was to make note of his initial discomfort and immediately ask himself what was going on for him. He would've had his answer at that point and would have dealt with his feelings then. However, as he wasn't used to acknowledging his finer feelings, he carried on as usual and took the familiar route of getting furious as a way of covering up the emotions that made him feel more exposed and insecure.

Sam could have recognised his original, more manageable feelings by "listening" to what his body was telling him. I know that could sound weird, but it really does work, and it's almost fool-proof. How many of you can remember instances where you felt your jaw clamp, or your stomach clench, or your legs start to tense? How many times have you gotten a headache or a backache because of something that happened during the day? How many of you have (or have had) nervous twitches which would start off when you were feeling particularly low? These are all signs from your inner self trying to tell you that you've disregarded something which did actually matter to you.

You know that expression, "the body never lies"? Well, when you're treating yourself badly and not giving yourself the care and consideration you deserve, your body is going to try to do its utmost to get your attention.

If you're not sure you'll be able to listen to your actual body at first, then another way of knowing that you've got a whole bunch of feelings at play is when you start to feel tired, depressed or stressed. These are warnings that all is not right and that you would be good for some well-needed TLC. It doesn't really matter if you can't figure out which feelings are trying to make themselves felt through your body's feedback, at least not when you first start trying to see what they are. What counts more is that, at long last, you're heeding the signs. That's already a massive step in the right direction! The rest will come gradually, just as long as you remember to look out for yourself.

Just so that you can understand what I'm really on about, here are a couple of examples which highlight how the body can tell you so much about what's going on for you if you're aware of its role as an alarm. I'm sure many of you will be able to think of times when they felt some discomfort in their body, but did as we all tend to do: completely ignored it! Come on, have you ever actually stopped what you were doing when you felt that hollow appear in the pit of your stomach; or did you carry right on with whatever was going on around you regardless?

> *Laura felt her stomach clench when her mother said "Oh, what would **you** know anyway?" She went straight into her usual coping mechanism, which was to start an argument with her mother. Laura didn't even recognise the fact that her mother was belittling her (which was a strong feeling) because she was so used to it, and she certainly wasn't aware of the fact that it stung so much because it made her feel unloved and judged (finer feelings). Beginning to argue was her way of burying all of her feelings so that she wouldn't notice the pain of feeling rejected.*

Or:

> *John felt his legs tense when his brother started making de-*

rogatory comments about him in front of his friends. As they were all older than him, he didn't dare stick up for himself, but the tenseness in his legs and the hollow in his gut were telling him that his feelings were being hurt. He started to tell himself that he probably was the useless nobody that his brother was making him out to be. After all, his friends were all joining in, so maybe they were right and he really was a loser.

Not being able to recognise what was really going on for him, which was that he felt persecuted by his brother and unhappy about what he was saying (strong feelings), as it made him feel inadequate and scorned (finer feelings), John took what had become the more comfortable route of berating himself and telling himself he probably deserved it. This was less painful than sensing his finer feelings.

In both of these scenarios, if Laura and John had been used to feeling their finer feelings they would have dealt with the situation differently. Their feelings wouldn't have had to build up to the stronger versions which then influenced them to reach for their usual coping mechanisms: attack mode (in Laura's case), or putting himself down (John). They would have recognised that their boundaries of what was tolerable and essential to their well-being were being violated and, in an assertive manner, they would have defined them and asked that they be respected by the other people before the scenarios spun into ones which became harmful to them.

∞∞∞∞∞∞

When you get really good at being in touch with your finer feelings, then you'll be able to do something which seems to be classified information (did I forget to tell you I used to be part of MI5?). This well-kept secret is that ***you can actually control and change your feelings.***

I promised you that I would let you in on this, but earlier on in this chapter was too soon. It's not a concept you can begin to understand when feelings are just some notion of which you have heard but haven't actually had any conscious experience! If you don't know what your feelings really are anymore, how could you be expected to think that you might be able to influence them in any way?

Feelings can seem so overwhelming, painful or disturbing that often they can completely take us over as though they were an independent part of our body and mind. However, as I've found out for myself with practice, I am "miraculously" in charge of my feelings (if I want to be), and not the other way around.

When you're genuinely in touch with your feelings and are used to acknowledging them as they appear, then you can start to influence and change them to suit you. You no longer live feelings as sensations which are separate to you and over which you have no leverage or control. As they arise you notice them immediately and so their element of surprise is lost. Once you have this new awareness of your feelings, you can then decide what you're going to do about them. They no longer take you over and now resume their original role: as a friendly reminder that you're in a situation which you're not enjoying and need to do something about. When you put yourself in charge of your feelings, this is when you truly start to realise how you can transform your life. If you can govern them, then you take charge of anything...

∞∞∞∞∞

Feelings and how to influence them

The way we've been brought up and then our ongoing lives as adults can really regulate our feelings, as they're based on our experience of life and what we've come to expect of it. For instance, if we're used to being spoken to badly, then we can more easily imagine that someone might be insulting us when no insult was intended. Or we might overreact to a situation and feel scared, when in fact there's nothing to be frightened of, or perhaps feel criticised at another moment when this wasn't the intention at all.

As you can see, when we're used to having more bad feelings in our lives than good, we find that our thoughts and behaviours are controlled by them. They can make us behave in a way that, were we in a healthier frame of mind, we would choose to abstain from. They might make us take decisions or do things that aren't necessarily beneficial to us or to others, but we do them anyway, because they help us escape the negative feelings that have arisen and we feel better for a while.

As such, and as we have seen previously, if we're used to negating our feelings (or having them undermined), they can become distorted in the same way as our needs once were. If we're more in touch with ourselves and we no longer have as much negative baggage to carry around, then:

1. We're going to be aware of our feelings when they rise up.
2. We're more likely to be able to pay attention to them when they do appear.
3. They're probably going to be a truer reflection of what's going on for us, and won't be coloured by our history or our beliefs.

When we begin to be able to do all three of the points mentioned above, we move on to being able to influence our feelings before they take **us** over. This course of action is of course more valid with regards to the negative feelings that you might have. (You don't want to be changing the effect that positive feelings will give you, you want to bring them on!) In a nutshell, it means that if a negative feeling comes up, once you've taken stock of why it's there, then you can decide what to do with it.

For instance:

- You can see if it's a feeling that's requesting your attention because something that isn't healthy for you is going on. You can then deal with the circumstances immediately, which will cancel the negative feeling.
- You can see if it's a feeling that's still warranted, or if it's based on a past experience which you have started to sort out in your head and for which the feeling is no longer as valid.
- You can feel the feeling and decide if it's a proper summary of the situation.
  If it is an old coping mechanism which is no longer necessary, *then you can decide to react by evaluating the event in a different light*. This will allow you to bring up a different, more positive feeling that you **have** chosen and which corresponds better to the situation. (Do you see here how the element of control comes into play? It just takes a change in your mindset, and hey presto!)
- And, as another example of how just changing the way you view the event can completely alter the set of corresponding feelings, you can sense the negative feeling and either decide that you'll let it ruin your day, or you can acknowledge it and then *LET IT GO*.

OMG! Let go of a feeling like that? One of those that, yesteryear, you might well have wrapped around you like a warm, woolly, comfortable blanket of depression, helplessness and distress? Strange how we tend to be gluttons for punishment and will keep hold of these negative feelings, as though in a funny sort of way we're almost validated by them! Unfortunately, we tend to welcome them as they're usually the confirmation we subconsciously seek for how rotten we feel, how badly we are being treated, and how much our life sucks! They understand us, at least, and rise to console us when no-one else does!

Well, it's time to **kick them out**, and here's how.

How to do it examples

I've given the following scenarios as a way of helping you to get a clearer understanding of how simple it can be to regulate your feelings. This is especially viable when you begin to get awareness of where the feelings might come from. As you start to know yourself better, through setting up boundaries and acknowledging your needs and feelings, this will become increasingly easy to do.

> *Cynthia had been abused as a child, which had made it very difficult for her to trust other people, particularly older men. In certain contexts, such as at work, when her manager (an older man) was asking her to do something that she didn't really want to do, it would unconsciously take her back to the time of her abuse. She would start to feel frightened, her pulse would race and she would be out of breath. She would begin to feel helpless and intimidated.*
>
> *As Cynthia knew that this childhood abuse had left her with a psychological scar, she was quick to tune in when her body*

started alerting her that she was beginning to feel uncomfortable. She would connect immediately with her finer feelings of powerlessness and being threatened and would start to reassure herself. She knew that these feelings were reminding her that she was being requested to do something she found disagreeable, and not that she was in danger. She chose to listen to her finer feelings and went to talk to her boss to see if there wasn't another approach that would work just as well.

Nathalie had had a teacher at school who was particularly unpleasant, and who put her down regularly in front of the whole class. At the time, this had created feelings of shame and distress which she hadn't known how to deal with as a child. As she got older, whenever these feelings would rise up, Nathalie would start to become almost hyperactive. She would take on as much work as possible and start compulsively cleaning her house. All this activity would keep her too busy to think, and she wouldn't have to sense these hurtful feelings.

When she met her husband, he often teased her about her OCD, and she had started to realise that she did it when she was feeling particularly stressed. It was the stress that reminded her of how she'd felt as a child. These days, when the feelings come up, Nathalie understands what's going on for her and chooses to not start being obsessive, even when the compulsion's there. She's able to reason and reassure herself, until this need fades.

Guy felt himself begin to get depressed. He knew that it was because he'd given his all to the race and although he'd trained for months and kept to his restrictive and unsatisfying food regime, it had all been for nothing. However, Guy also knew that starting to feel down was his coping mechanism for his feelings of inadequacy, and so he listened immediately when he felt himself become pessimistic. He gave himself a couple of hours to feel sad because he knew he had to acknowledge what was going on for him, but after that he told himself that he'd done his best and he started to shift his mood towards feeling more hopeful. The depression didn't last, because Guy had paid attention to it and allowed himself to feel his sadness before moving on.

With these examples you can see that as you get to know yourself better, you literally can choose how you allow your feelings to influence you and your take on the world. Suddenly, they can be seen as the friend and ally that they were always destined to be. They serve as a timely reminder that we need to pay attention to, and give more to ourselves, and they no longer have the role of a hurtful companion that we would just like to bury and forget.

When you haven't been used to acknowledging them, you're not able to understand why certain feelings come up, nor to what they're referring. As a result, they tend to take you over: you either keep dumbing yourself down so that you feel less and less, or you do the opposite and have violent reactions that are triggered by them. Either way, this doesn't make for a life of positivity and joy.

When you start to truly relate with your inner thoughts you'll know why certain feelings are there and you'll be able to talk yourself through them, rather than have automatic, unconscious reactions to those feelings. Then you can deliberately give yourself the reassurance and support that you need, which will help you to resolve the situation immediately. When you hear yourself and start to honour your feelings, it will allow you to fall back in love with yourself, and your world view will change with it. When you actually *like* who you are, you see the world through different eyes, and life starts to feel more enjoyable and colourful and satisfying.

It's actually much simpler than you might've thought, isn't it?

Now that you've started listening to your gentle inner voice, there's another one that you'll probably have to silence, because given half a chance it'll take you over completely. This is the voice of the critic and it takes no prisoners!

Chapter 4

Inner critic: who is that person in my head?

Many of us have got this person living in our head. We don't know where it (I'm going to call this person "it" because it can either be a man or a woman, but also because it doesn't deserve any name other than "IT"!) came from, we don't know why it's there and we sure as heck would like it to leave...

The inner critic is the worst person in the world to live with because it will never give you a break. It's like a vulture who perches on your shoulder and pecks incessantly right into your squishy skull!

Your inner critic doesn't ever want to give you a rest and will be ready with a derogatory comment or a cold-hearted judgement at any time of the day or night. Demoralising doesn't even begin to sum up the effect that the critic can have on you. If there were a crush-me competition it would win all the trophies and then wave them in your face as yet more confirmation of how appallingly worthless you are!

So where does this critic really come from?

Society isn't always kind and has conspired to help create an internal critic in many of us. As children we might've had parents who couldn't help but point out what they thought needed improving in us. You know the kind of remarks: "What's wrong with you?" or "Maybe that wasn't a good idea..." or "Now look what you've done!" or "You could've done better." They might not have meant some of the comments uncaringly, and perhaps thought they were helping us. But if any of you felt your shoulders tense, or your stomach constrict, or your spirits droop, then you know that you were living these statements negatively.

Even small comments like, "Go and wash your hair!" or "Change your clothes, they're not smart enough/clean enough/appropriate" would have had an insidious impact on our self-esteem. We could have interpreted this as meaning that **we** were not "good enough," that perhaps our judgement was not to be trusted, something was wrong with us physically, or our parents were ashamed of us. There seems to be no end to the tricks that our internal voice is prepared to play in order to make us feel awful.

At school we might have come across other ways of being belittled. Who hasn't been the brunt of playground whispers on at least one occasion? Or you might have had a teacher who used "humour" as a way of censuring you. And just in case you weren't already feeling rubbish enough, on a general level, ads and the TV are continuously showing you what "perfection" is and unfortunately, most of us don't seem even close to it, either physically or in our achievements!

What happens over time is that we start to develop our own inner critic who is more than willing to step in on most occasions and give us as hard a time as it possibly can. In fact, this voice can get so loud that it can become the only thing that you can hear, and it goes on and on... And when it can't find anything to criticise about you *(really?!)* then it can usually turn and find someone else to harangue. It's exhausting living with the critic, as those of you who have one will know. It just seems to never let up.

Identifying the Inner Critic

The critic has many disguises, and it uses them well so that you may never be able to rip off its mask and find the sad, frightened person behind it. It's good at dodging and diving and will keep you on your toes, giving you the hard time you think you deserve. But do you?

As we've seen, those of us with a strong internal voice will have "grown" it as a result of our experiences as children. It quite often resembles the voices of our parents, and we convince ourselves that if we listen to it we'll become a better person who will more easily get other people's love and approval. The job of the inner critic is to make you acceptable to yourself and others, and it does this by using a few choice methods of chastisement which we buy into because our self-esteem is already very fragile, if not almost non-existent.

Many of us also choose to develop this defamer of ourselves because we can use it as a form of damage limitation. After all, if we get in there first with the condemning, then at least we're dishing out the dirt before anyone else does, and we can hand out what we want! Having a critic becomes "safe;" at least, it's a way of being we are familiar with, and it leaves us feeling more secure as we know it can be relied upon to always be there for us. Crazy, isn't it, the modes of behaviour we can use to try to make ourselves feel better?

So what does the critic have hidden in its Mary Poppins bag of tricks to make you feel inadequate? (Please don't take what I've put below personally, by the way, I'm just trying to accentuate how awful it is to live with an inner critic... And I like to think I'm funny!)

Shoulds – You "should" do this and you "should" do that. The list of shoulds is generally endless and is designed to make you feel like the useless human being that you are. Musts and oughts are also friends with shoulds, and they *should* all be chucked out the same window!

Mistakes – You aren't allowed to make them. Only complete dunces and lowlifes make mistakes and obviously you must be one of them (no surprise there!) because you make them all the time. You probably *should* think more seriously about digging that hole to hide yourself in.

Perfection – You know that it's not acceptable unless it's perfect, and yet everything you do seems to go the same route. You *must* be doing it on purpose! Why can't you just get it right, for once in your life?

Criticism – You're only doing it for your own good. It's to make you a better person, someone who's at least worth having around. After all, if you're not there setting yourself straight, you're going to be going through life doing just anything, any old how. You're your own best friend, and don't you forget it!

Blame – You're right to keep going on at yourself. After all, if I were you I'd also be feeling pointless. And when you felt bad the other day you should have, because after all it's all your fault anyway. Why are you so incompetent and hopeless and just plain pointless?

Guilt – You know you *should* feel guilty. Already all these other things are so wrong with you, and then you didn't help that man when his bag fell over... I know you had your hands full, but you *ought* to have helped anyway. I mean, how many times do things like this have to happen before you get it right?

Warned you I was going to get carried away! I definitely didn't want to make you feel worse, but now that my own internal critic has been retired (almost), it was really fun to bring it back to life for a while. **There's nothing like a blast from the past!**

A lot of what I wrote up there were situations I experienced first-hand from my inner critic. It was always having a go about anything and everything. When it ran out of steam about me, then it would usually turn on the next unsuspecting victim it laid its eyes on. Even people walking by in the street could be in for a bashing! So if you've got one, you have my full-hearted support as you begin to get rid of it for good.

So as we saw above, these are the tricks that the inner critic uses against us that make us feel bad some of the time and terrible for more of it. When we've been used to this mode of operating for a while, the critic is very rarely quiet and we become used to having it in full flow for most of our waking moments.

Because we're into self-harm (of the mental kind), we accept this voice and don't stop to consider either its verity or its validity. It has so become a part of our life that we think this is how most people go through theirs. It's only when this voice ceases that we can actually realise how omnipresent and cruel it was. The relief when we stop the voice with its incessant cutting backchat cannot even be described, but imagine coming out of a tunnel that's just suffered a major explosion and I think you'll get the general idea...

∞∞∞∞∞

The wrath of the critic

Now that we've looked at the more minor ways that the inner critic can manifest in your life, it's time to get serious and look at what happens when it gathers steam. When it really gets going, this inner criticism can take even more vicious forms which are so detrimental to our well-being I could weep. There are three main ways that this can take place and you might find that you have a finger in every pie (lucky you!), or that you seem to focus a lot of energy in just one area.

To evaluate the critic's influence on you, see if you find yourself doing any of the following:

Distorting reality

This is a very painful mode of operating which is highly limiting for those who do it. Unconsciously reading things which aren't there into a situation is extremely harmful to your well-being and will always stop you from feeling serene, confident and hopeful. How can you possibly enjoy life or grab hold of it with enthusiasm and anticipation when you're experiencing a warped view of it?

Do any of these (or similar) apply to you?

- You walk into a room and think that everyone's going to look at you and find something negative to say.
- You think that when you start talking people are going to walk away or find you boring.
- You take it personally when someone makes a comment about a situation. Even if you have nothing to do with it, you'll think it's aimed at you.
- You're quicker to see the negative in a situation than the positive.
- You over-generalise. You use vocabulary like "always" or "everything" or "never."
- You see yourself as a victim: "It always happens to me" or "What have I done to deserve this?"
- You feel like your life is ruined when something (even insignificant) goes wrong or doesn't happen.
- You're convinced you can imagine what other people are thinking (mostly about you).
- You have unrealistic expectations: a party has to be amazing or you don't enjoy any of it; your boss has to give you unlimited praise or he hates you, etc.
- You assume that most people react and think about things the same way that you do.

Catastrophic Predictions

This is like walking around with a heavy load all day and all night. You won't be able to live life to its fullest when you anticipate that most situations are going to have a negative outcome. It would take a huge amount of courage to be able to aspire to anything when your expectation of life and what it brings is pessimistic and you foresee failure and rejection at every turn. Life is so dark when we live with catastrophic predictions.

Do any of these (or similar) apply to you?

- You think that if you say no, the person will never speak to you again.
- You think that if you affirm your boundaries the person will leave you.
- You think that if you show your feelings you'll be called selfish and will be ignored.
- You think that if you try to initiate sex you will be rejected.
- You think that if you make a joke no-one will laugh.
- You think you'll be ridiculed if you put yourself forward in any way.
- You think that if you don't give in you'll be shunned forever.
- You think it's best to not even try, because it's all going to go pear-shaped anyway.
- You think there's no point in asking because the answer will be no.
- You think the same could happen to you, whenever you hear bad news.
- You expect to fail and make mistakes and think they'll be catastrophic and the consequences will be huge. There is no middle ground.

Core Beliefs

Core beliefs constitute your convictions about who you are as a person. Most of us will have at least a few core beliefs that we have been given by others, or that over time we have awarded ourselves. They are incredibly limiting and debilitating. We're so used to living by their dictates that we probably don't ever review their validity, or are no longer necessarily aware of their existence. We live under their shadow and it makes for a life of restriction and poor self-esteem.

Do any of these (or similar) apply to you?

- You think if something goes wrong it's because you deserve it.
- You think if you can't answer a question it's because you're stupid.
- You think if you haven't got a boy/girlfriend it's because you're ugly and uninteresting.
- You think if you have bad luck it's because you're doomed.
- You think if you break something it's because you're clumsy.
- You think if you try you won't succeed, as you're a failure.
- You think you're bad at a particular subject because you're useless.
- You think no-one would listen to you because you're worthless.
- You think you're not loveable.

Well, that should be enough to be getting on with. This chapter is turning out to be mighty depressing, so here's something to cheer you up!

Just so that you can really get a sense of how these three ways of operating can play out and affect your capacity to enjoy life, to feel comfortable and happy, here are some examples that will help to demonstrate them:

> *Owen had just got a phone call from someone he'd met at a business diner. The person had called to ask him if they could meet up to discuss some of the points which Owen had raised during the diner. After his initial pleasant surprise, Owen's inner voice started up and said, "He must have got the wrong*

guy. You're such a fraud, you'll never be able to keep it up for long enough. What if he really knows his stuff? He'll see through you immediately, and then what will you do? You can't keep a conversation going for that long; you're just not sufficiently skilled and capable."

Owen started to feel very nervous and decided that he needed to phone the guy back and cancel their meeting. What was going on here was Owen started to feel insecure, which had the knock-on effect of then allowing the critic to pipe up and submerge him with talk about his supposed inadequacies. Of course, Owen wasn't incompetent, but having the critic chime in meant that he could cover the disagreeable feelings of anxiety which these doubts brought up in him. He only gave himself over to listening to the critic because that made him feel safer than thinking about going to the meeting.

In this instance, Owen was using all three concepts. He distorted reality by thinking the man had phoned the wrong person. He had an automatic catastrophic prediction when he envisioned the meeting going badly. And he used one of his core beliefs about himself, which was that he was inadequate.

Isabelle knew that it was best to let it go when Marc started getting annoyed with her. She started to feel her stomach tense and then her inner voice started up with its usual refrain of "Why can't you just keep quiet? You're always stirring things up and ruining them. I don't know why he stays with you, anyone else would have given up years ago. Anyway, leave it now or he might walk out, and then where would you be?"

This voice was one which Isabelle had adopted from her father. When she had been growing up, whenever she'd tried to say what she thought and needed, her father would start telling her off by saying things like, "You're always going on about something. You're so demanding. I don't know why we put up with you. We should send you to boarding school to get some peace and quiet. No-one is going to put up with this when you grow up."

Her core beliefs had been completely distorted by what her father told her. Isabelle now believed that she was unpleasant and difficult to live with. As a result, she was in a relationship with a man who wasn't treating her properly, but she believed that her needs were not reasonable and she allowed herself to be mistreated because she feared being abandoned.

Here, Isabelle was using two out of three concepts. She had a catastrophic prediction when she thought Marc would walk out on her if she said anything, and some of her core beliefs rose up and reminded her that she was probably being unreasonable. If you dug deeper you would find another core belief which was that she wasn't loveable, either, and could be deserted if she made too many requests.

Facing life with these three ways of functioning as your companions won't make living a joyful experience. If you don't have inner resources such as self-love and self-esteem then life will seem more difficult and less fulfilling; it will become an ordeal that's gloomy and discouraging. Ditching these ways of being is vital if you wish to give yourself a life that is kind and gentle and caring.

> Just for the fun of it, here's one that happened to me just now. As I was writing this on the computer, I clicked on the wrong page and opened the internet, not Word. The voice popped up immediately with, "Typical, you can't even do that right." HILARIOUS! I couldn't believe it was happening!

> The difference is: my inner critic doesn't sound as nasty as it used to, I heard it straight away and laughed out loud because of the timing, and then I kicked that nasty old critic right out. To be fair, it hardly ever pops up these days and I dismiss it immediately, but it's something you have to be aware of: we are never fully "cured" and keeping your inner critic in check is a life-long process.

∞∞∞∞∞

Silencing Your Inner Critic

What, therefore, can be put in place to shut the critic up forever? 'Cos after all of that, I'm sure you need to know that there's something that can be done about it.

What really worked for me was talking back to the critic. I could only start to do this once I'd begun to work on my boundaries and was getting back in touch with my needs and feelings. The process of self-validation is of the utmost importance at this stage. There's no way you're going to be able to talk back to such a powerful critic if you haven't started believing in, and being at least a little kinder to yourself.

My critic came from being put down a lot as a child, so I naturally thought that I wasn't a good or nice person. I was always being told how difficult I was and my childhood was one of conflict and verbal abuse. My inner critic was a voice of self-loathing, but there are all sorts of voices out there.

So what really packs a punch when you're talking back to your critic is being able to identify whose voice it is in the first place. If it's not yours, then it's all the easier to be able to tell it to shut up!

Beatrice heard the critic sound off the minute she got offered the promotion. "You'll never manage. Best not to even try. You'll be out of a job in five seconds flat."

However, Beatrice had learned to recognise this voice and she knew that it had started up because of the new challenge. It reminded her of when she was a child and how her mother would get very nervous each time Beatrice would attempt something new. She could still hear her mother saying, "You won't be able to manage it and you'll fall off!" on the day she learnt to ride her bike. Or the time that she went to try out for the basketball team and her mother had said, "They only want really sporty people who can run fast. You don't stand a chance and you shouldn't try out."

Beatrice's problem with the critic only arose when she was in situations that took her out of her comfort zone. If it hadn't been for her mother, she wouldn't have had a problem with the challenge. As she knew it was her mother's voice and not her own, she was able to talk back to the critic and reassure it that she knew what she was doing and was more than capable of accepting and succeeding in this fresh opportunity.

Jake had grown up with a father who was hardly ever there, and when he was, he spent most of his time locked away in his office. When Jake would go and see him, his father would look up, tell him he was disturbing him and ask him to leave. As a result, Jake had created a core belief that it was because he wasn't loveable that his father had never made the time to talk with him, hug him or tuck him in at night. This had led him to have a series of unhealthy relationships in which he didn't affirm himself and was treated badly.

> *He'd grown out of this core belief when he got married and had children of his own. Jake realised that his father had just chosen to not make time for him, and it had nothing to do with him or his qualities as a person: he was perfectly loveable, as his wife and children showed him.*
>
> Jake understood that his father had put his busy life first and that having a child was not a priority for him, so when his inner voice spoke up telling him that he wasn't loveable, he was able to talk back to it saying that this wasn't true until it eventually gave up.

Another good way of plucking up the courage to talk back to your critic is by asking yourself if what the inner critic says is true. This is when you really can put all your flaky beliefs to the test.

> *When you start telling yourself that you're mean, ask yourself: is this true?*
> *Wait a bit to see what comes up. Are you telling yourself that, or are you hearing other people's voices?*
> *Ask yourself again, is it true?*
> *Find examples where you know for a fact that you behaved in a way that was kind or generous or gentle.*
> *Where is the mean person? Is he or she really there?*

By re-evaluating what the critic says, you're able to put things into perspective and that's when you can start getting rid of the negative effects of the critic on your mind. You'll be popping myths faster than you can say "Begone, devil spawn!"

> *What about those times when you beat yourself up for being clumsy, stupid, a bad parent, rubbish at your job, always late, irresponsible... Ask yourself if these things are true.*
>
> *Wait and see what comes up and then ask yourself again if they are true.*

> *Find examples of when you weren't like that and sit with them, let them wash over you and when the voice of doubt comes up, tell it, "No way, I've got examples! I'm not listening to you anymore! JUST SHUT UP."*

You'll have to keep telling your inner critic to be quiet, get lost, stop talking tosh; whatever works for you. But like most playground bullies, when you start standing up to them, they back down. You'll be amazed by how quickly you're able to get that voice to leave you alone. It will take a bit of time, you might find yourself saying "shut up" a thousand times a day, but one day you'll realise that you haven't had to say it in the last 10 minutes; then 20; then 40... Peace at last.

Or you can do it by watching your thoughts as they circle round and round in your head. Really feel how they make you respond; sense their effect on your body and on your state of mind. Rather than letting them just meander through your mind, choose to concentrate on them and what they're saying. And then just tell them to STOP! Turn them off. Then wait and see what happens.

What you should sense is that the world doesn't go into a tail spin, you don't disappear into a puff of smoke, BUT your thoughts suddenly just don't exist anymore and therefore can't impact you... They've totally lost their mesmerising hold on you.

Try this each time you start going round in circles in your head and you'll soon realise that these are just thoughts. They used to have a grip on you when you believed in them, but now you're beginning to understand that if you don't want to listen to them or give them power over you, then they cannot survive. You can finally understand that they were just thought forms, not solid reality. The only thing that made them real was you allowing them to be.

How to do it examples

If you're going to be successful at beating off the critic, it's best to attend to the three most destructive forces behind its voice: distorting reality, catastrophic predictions and core beliefs. The other tricks of the trade (shoulds, mistakes, blame, guilt etc.) will take care of themselves once you're consciously dealing with the critic.

Before attempting any of the exercises below, write a non-exhaustive list (yes, please keep adding to it all the time) of all your good qualities and positive points. You'll need some ammunition to keep the critic at bay and it's best to have it prepared beforehand (at least at the beginning) so that you can answer it quickly before you allow doubt to set in.

Distorting Reality

When you distort reality, then you're no longer able to see situations as they actually are. There are many tricks of the trade for doing this and you may recognise some that you use: black and white thinking (it's all one way, or it's all the other; there's no middle ground), only seeing the negative, over-generalising, personalising, concluding that things **are** the way you feel them to be, assuming blame or guilt, reading minds (lucky you!).

When the critic pops up with any of these, call its bluff. For instance:

- In the case of negative thinking: when you catch yourself doing it, ask yourself if there isn't another way of seeing things. Do *not* let yourself off the hook, there's always more than one way of viewing things and your job is to make sure it's not negative.
- Over-generalising also is a bad habit, so when you catch

yourself using "always", "never" etc. pull yourself up, acknowledge that this is not necessarily the case, and then consciously phrase it another way.
- And as far as being psychic is concerned, remember that you didn't even know what your finer feelings were, so when you hear yourself presuming to know what other people are going to be thinking and saying about you: *just don't.* You have no idea, so imagine instead that they might actually have only positive things to say, or worst case, nothing at all!

Catastrophic Predictions

Dealing with catastrophic predictions can also be fun. When you start poking holes in them you'll see how easily they deflate. What you'll be left wondering is how you could have fooled yourself into believing them for so long. These predictions usually seem more grotesque as you concentrate on them – this is when you know for sure that you have a very vivid imagination.

> *Joan had been called up for a job interview. As the date approached, she felt herself getting worried and tense. As the interview got closer, these sensations turned to disaster scenarios. She started wondering what would happen if she was asked a question she couldn't answer. Would she just sit there, red-faced, hoping the ground would swallow her up? Would the manager start looking at her as though she was a fool? Would he ask her to leave, as she was wasting his time?*
>
> *She got herself totally wound up in a very unlikely storyline which stemmed from her insecurity and lack of self-confidence.*

In order to deal with this catastrophic prediction which otherwise might stop her from going to the interview, Joan had to ask herself some logical questions that she just couldn't dodge around, such as:

- What is the likelihood of not being able to answer?
- Is it probable that her face would go red and if so, would it matter? People are allowed to be nervous in interviews. The manager would be sure to understand and not think anything of it, or she could even make light of it.
- What are the chances that he would ask her to leave? That really would be very extreme! She knew she was good at what she did and she had as much of a chance of getting this job as anyone.

When you stop listening to the negative refrain and start taking the scenario apart, you know that it's totally illogical and just fuelled by fear, nerves or self-doubt. When you get good at it, you'll be laughing out loud at how mad some of your thoughts were.

The examples I've just given for distorting reality and catastrophic predictions are quite clear cut and show just what a major impact they can have on our everyday life. But there are many times where they're more subtle and act rather like the slow drip of the tap which you don't notice until suddenly there's a deluge... You can probably relate to this, it's the kind of scenario which starts with one small thought, that just keeps growing and coming back at you.

For instance: if you'd just said "no" to someone for a change, you might then spend a lot of time ruminating about how they were going to be the next time you meet. You might start off imagining them coming in pulling a face, but over the course of the day, the scenario will amplify until you imagine them coming in slamming doors and ignoring you, or screaming and shouting, or packing their stuff and leaving... The scenario snakes around in your mind getting more catastrophic and distorted by the second... You know the ones I mean; they're really crazy!

Core Beliefs

This is the destructive force which I personally think affects us the most. If you weren't weighed down by negative core beliefs, then I think there would probably be less chance that catastrophic predictions and distorting reality would be able to exert such a hold on you. So evaluate which one is the most recurrent for you, but if you only have time to work on one then this would be it for me.

The best way to find out what your core beliefs are is to pay attention to your thoughts when you experience something negative. It would be a good idea to track this (a little bit of paper time) until you begin to get a clear idea, otherwise you'll tend to forget.

When you feel inadequate, stressed or angry, listen to your immediate surrounding thoughts.

- *If you regularly hear the same kind of thought such as: "you're a loser," "you're a waste of space" or "you'll never get anywhere," then you're dealing with a core belief that could be about your potential for accomplishment, or lack of self-worth or lack of self-esteem.*
- *If the voice tells you "you're bad," "you're a rotten person" or "you're a useless human being," then your core belief could be that you're not loveable, cannot be accepted by others or that you're insignificant.*

Of course, you'll have to work out for yourself what the basis for your core belief(s) might be, but watching your thoughts and seeing a repeated pattern will help you to sort out what they are and where they come from. After that, you can use the same techniques as those you learnt in Chapter 3 about your feelings: ask yourself if these beliefs are valid, if they're based in the past, or if they were ever true in the first place. Give yourself examples of why it's not true, repeat them over and over, then let your attachment to this belief go. Your stomach might lurch at the thought, but now that you know how you've been sabotaging yourself with these core beliefs, you owe it to yourself to release them.

Don't worry if it doesn't happen overnight, but the more you talk back to your critic, the quieter it will become. It only occupied so much space because you allowed it to. Now tell him/her their time is over and **you** are taking back control: you're going to fill yourself up with good thoughts, healthy beliefs and sunny scenarios!

Chapter 5

Self-esteem: oh, I remember that!

This leaves us with the final instalment of how to get back in touch with yourself. By now you may be finding that after many years in the wilderness, you've come across someone whom you really rather like and who is in the process of becoming a confident, happy and blossoming human being. It's actually quite simple, really, you just needed a gentle nudge in the right direction and the rest, as they say, takes care of itself. Actually, I think we can't help ourselves after a while because it all starts to feel so ***great*** you just want to keep getting more of the same.

So now we come to your self-esteem which, for a number of years, has probably been taking a real beating; but as we've seen throughout this book, we don't really need to wonder why. It's clear that the original reasons for your lack of self-esteem might not have much to do with you, but if you then go on to refuse yourself some, or all of the things that are basic necessities for living a life of satisfaction and fulfilment (boundaries, needs etc.) then it's really rather self-explanatory. The upshot of this however, is that as you've been becoming increasingly aware of the whys and wherefores of what's been going on for you and now have the "tools" to promote your well-being, the circle towards greater psychological health is nearly complete.

Self-esteem comes about and grows as a natural response to

nurturing, kindness and love. When we deny ourselves that or accept it when others give us less than that, then we cannot have good self-esteem no matter how hard we might try. The magical thing about introducing the 4 other elements to ourselves is that our self-esteem will begin to develop spontaneously, which means that at last we get to the stage in the book where we finally won't have **TO DO AS MUCH WORK!** Another totally amazing thing is that when others see you treating yourself with care and respect, then they can't help but do the same thing. It couldn't get much better than that, now, could it?

Where does low self-esteem come from?

Again self-esteem (or lack thereof) comes from our childhood and our experiences and treatment from parents, siblings, other adults and our peers. We know that our self-esteem isn't great when we ask ourselves, "Who am I, and what do I feel (or say) about myself?" and all we seem to get is a bunch of negatives or some umming and ahhing. When we genuinely like ourselves, we can get very enthusiastic at the thought of describing ourselves, as our confidence levels are high and we feel positive about who we are. Those of us with low self-esteem, however, will tend to give negative evaluations about ourselves and what we do.

Just to gauge where you think you might place yourself on the self-esteem evaluation scale, I've given you a few ideas of the kinds of questions you could ask to help you assess how you view yourself:

- Do you value yourself?
- Do you feel valued by others?
- Do you accept yourself, or do you find things to criticise and berate?
- Are you able to list all of your inner qualities and take pride in them?
- Are you able to list your less attractive traits and accept (not necessarily excuse) them as a part of who you are?
- Do you validate all your accomplishments, even the small ones, and see them as a sign of how great you are?
- Do you feel enthusiastic about who you are?
- Do you feel positive about what you do?

When we were children, if we didn't receive the proper nurture, approval and support which we should all get as human beings, then we're more likely to actively seek it from others as we get older because we need this validation of ourselves that we didn't get when we were young. People who didn't receive this confirmation of their worth are less likely to approve of, and believe in, themselves. They don't feel endorsed on the inside, where it counts the most, and so they increasingly look for it or demand it from the outside.

People who have low self-esteem are more likely to have received this kind of treatment as children:

- Physical, sexual or mental abuse.
- Verbal abuse, criticism, put downs, denigration.
- Withdrawal of approval or affection, shown by being ignored or manipulated.
- Bullying or excessive control.
- Being ridiculed.
- Expected to be "perfect" and belittled when they aren't.
- Made to feel that they're not good enough.
- Absent parents who make up for the neglect by spoiling

and not giving their children boundaries which make them feel secure.

Having read this list, I don't suppose you need any explanation as to how this sort of behaviour towards you could have such a devastating impact on your sense of Self. Anyone who's been on the receiving end of this kind of conduct has more than enough reasons to explain why they might have been finding life so difficult and unfulfilling. But the damage once done, can be undone. With the understanding of the past which you now have, you can free yourself and move forwards towards the creation of a present and future that offers you much more.

But it's not just those of us who were put down, or ignored, or not cared for correctly as children who might grow up with low self-esteem and the need to get endorsement from the outside. Some of us might have had a childhood in which we received a lot of love and approval but the fall comes when you meet someone who doesn't treat you as well as you're used to, or when experiences of life treat you harshly (severe illness, poor academic results, financial problems, redundancy, depression). Little by little your self-esteem will be eroded until you wind up at the same stage as the person who didn't have such a positive upbringing. The challenge is the same for both of you: you have to start building yourself up from the inside and forget about validation of your worth from outside sources.

If you find yourself doing any of the following then you have confirmation that your self-esteem probably is suffering:

- Hesitating until you get encouragement.
- Waiting for compliments which might never come.
- Wanting approval as a way of being reassured.
- Feeling sad when you don't get the acknowledgement

you would have liked.
- Handing over your personal power to others as a way of feeling accepted.
- Hiding your accomplishments to avoid the pain of not having them recognised.
- Feeling gutted (literally) when yet again you don't get any praise.
- Not putting yourself forward in any way.
- Minimising your needs and feelings, and therefore reducing yourself.
- Not feeling loveable.
- Finding yourself angry: either frequently close to the edge, or instantly boiling over.
- Feeling nervous when you are taken out of your comfort zone.

When we're not confident about ourselves then it does mean that we're likely to be either waiting for validation from others which might never come, or might not be in the form which we'd like it to be in. It also affects us because without being conscious of it we can demote ourselves and our value as a person. The first example below is actually about me (the name has been changed for confidentiality purposes!); I used to efface all trace of myself because I thought I was nothing. No trace = no person.

> *Elisa had cleared away all her belongings before leaving the house. She and Richard had had a huge argument the night before and she was still feeling unsure of herself. She preferred to hide all trace of her presence from him, as she felt that any reminder of her might make him furious again. She found it safer to pretend that she didn't exist as it made her feel less hollow inside.*

Or:

Victor was feeling very proud of the grades he'd achieved that term, but as he got closer to home, his feeling of satisfaction faded, the pit of his stomach started to ache and he began to feel quite down. He knew there wasn't much point telling his parents because they would pay little attention to what he was saying, much less show appreciation. By the time he got home, he felt very sad and decided not to run the risk of disappointment by telling them his results and not getting the validation he would like.

Or:

Since losing his job, Martin had found it very difficult to go out. As a result he was losing touch with his friends as he usually found excuses to not meet up with them. Over time they were giving up on him and were not contacting him as much. He was finding himself increasingly isolated.

∞∞∞∞∞

How low self-esteem affects your life

Many of our ways of adapting to low self-esteem are not conscious; we have all sorts of systems in place which we use when our already fragile self-regard is taking a knocking. Unfortunately, these methods only serve to reinforce our negative self-image, as they're either directly harmful to us or make us feel so bad that it can't help but adversely impact our self-esteem.

When we stop for a moment to evaluate the results of low self-esteem on our way of being, it can actually be quite frightening. It's so rare that we stop to measure the impact but when we do, we understand immediately how debilitating it can be.

Below you'll find different ways in which the effects of low self-esteem can be felt in our lives:

- Our relationships (be they friendships or our primary love relationship) will suffer and can be unfulfilling experiences that offer us little, and which are fraught with problems.
- Low self-esteem can affect the way you relate to others, with you either becoming a "victim" in relationships, or by not being able to form healthy links with other people. This is displayed through different kinds of emotional unavailability which, in its extreme form, can appear as narcissism or psychopathy. (This cannot be a subject for this book as it is very complex, but "*I'll be back*" on that one).
- Low self-esteem can impact our academic performance, or when we are older our job performance, not because we don't necessarily have the capacities, but because we sabotage ourselves by dumbing ourselves down, or not taking what we perceive to see as risks (trying for exams, aiming higher in our educational aspirations, going for better jobs or promotions, etc.).
- Low self-esteem can lead to abuses of all kinds such as: alcohol, drugs, sexual (including acting out), self-harm, overworking, gambling, over exercising, perfectionism...
- And in its more subtle form, it can lead (amongst other things) to stress, anxiety, anger, frustration, shame, guilt, isolation, neglect and depression.

I mean, did you fully realise that not believing in yourself or giving yourself care and love could have this sort of impact on your life? But not to worry, you're getting to a better place, and if it's the same for you as for me, I'm all the more appreciative of my way of being now because I have the past to compare it to. I hope it'll be the same for you as it will serve as confirmation that you're really on track and that things are definitely looking up.

Here are some examples that will help to demonstrate the consequences that low self-esteem can have:

> *Ellie looked down at her body in the shower and all she was aware of was a mass of wobbling, saggy flesh. All she could see was her stomach and thighs. She closed her eyes when it came to soaping herself because she couldn't bear to look anymore. She was hit by a wave of self-loathing so strong that it almost rocked her body. She knew that the only way to deal with this was to cut out the only meal she'd planned to eat that day. Her face looked pinched and wounded but she wasn't aware of that; she only felt the disgust.*

> *Carl knew that the date for the end of year exams was fast approaching and he felt a moment of intense anxiety because so far he'd done very little work towards them. He began to feel guilty because as the date got nearer he found himself withdrawing even more and doing even less; he just couldn't help himself. He began to feel depressed as this habitual pattern started to repeat.*

> *Since he'd been ill, Ian found it increasingly difficult to ask for help. His dependency on others disgusted him and as a result he found himself becoming more depressed. He was unable to verbalise what was going on for him because he would start to get angry straight away. He had started drinking more in order to numb himself.*

People with healthy self-esteem can have good days and bad days, the same as anyone else, but it's their bounce-back ability which is different. It's normal to have days where you're not so pleased, either about yourself or about life in general. Someone with good self-esteem will take the knocks and get back up more quickly, as they know that good times are just around the corner. Someone with low self-esteem will be more easily overwhelmed when times get tough, and their dislike of themselves will grow disproportionately. People with low self-esteem are personally affected by adverse events and will use them to enhance their lack of self-worth.

When we have good self-esteem, we're not only better able to assess ourselves realistically and give credit where it's due, but we're also able to look at the less favourable aspects of our being and not condemn ourselves for having them. We're able to acknowledge both our strengths and weaknesses and live comfortably with them, without debilitating self-judgement.

In the cases of Ellie, Carl and Ian, had their self-esteem been better, they wouldn't have reacted the way they did. Ellie wouldn't have fixated on those two areas of her body and seen them in such a distorted way. She would have been able to be more realistic about her body shape and would also have been able to compliment herself for other parts of her body which she liked much more. Either way, she wouldn't have gotten to a stage of such pronounced dislike of herself.

Carl wouldn't have found the familiar route of self-sabotage as he subconsciously stopped himself from working so as not to take the "risk" of trying and perhaps failing. The fact of reducing himself and his potential in this way was having an unmistakable effect on him and what might only be mild instances of depression at this stage in his life, would probably lead to a more severe form of depression later on.

Ian would have been able to see that no longer being able to fully care for himself without outside help was not a barrier to living a satisfying life. If he had better self-esteem he would not have rejected himself and his new circumstances. He would have been less angry and would have been able to create stronger bonds with those around him instead of seeking to anesthetise himself with alcohol.

∞∞∞∞∞

Low self-esteem and relationships

When you suffer from low self-esteem you can feel insignificant, unlovable and useless. You cannot help but see yourself in a negative light, and you have no real belief in your value as a human being or your capacities to strive and achieve. You may get to the stage where your self-esteem is so low that you think that no-one could like you or fall in love with you, or you may have given up any hope with regards to having a fulfilling life, either at work or at home.

Many of us who suffer from low self-esteem try to seek validation from others or, more unfortunately, *through* others. As a result we think that we acquire value only if it's provided through the eyes and words of other people. The knock-on effect of this for some of us is that we're more likely to invite relationships that aren't good for us. A part of us recognises the challenge of trying to get approval from the other person and we gravitate towards them as opposed to someone healthier. We feel that when we get it, we'll finally have all the validation that we've ever needed. Unfortunately, the only thing wrong with this scenario is that it's like trying to get water from a stone...

Yes, the rotten truth is that when you're in this type of relationship, the power play which goes on between the two of you means that one of you starts being a victim and accepting treatment and circumstances which aren't tolerable (approval seeker), while the other person becomes a persecutor (this can take many different guises). Either way, it's not healthy and it doesn't make for a fulfilling or happy relationship.

If you don't feel adequate, secure, capable or loveable, you can unconsciously expect the other person to fill this gap for you. People who enter into this sort of unwritten contract are also more likely to stay in this type of relationship, even though it's probably quite damaging. However, when you start to work on your self-esteem, you begin to fill this void for yourself. This brings you to a place which is far more empowering for you as you become self-sufficient about making yourself feel valued and appreciated.

(Again, I could say a lot about how lack of self-esteem does not only affect people who are seeking validation of themselves through others, it is equally important to those whose lack of self-esteem, lack of self-love and self-worth has caused them to become emotionally unavailable. They are quite often the partners of those who ask for approval from outside of themselves; but it really is too big a subject for this book.)

Here are some examples to clarify how lack of self-esteem can keep you in relationships that are detrimental to you:

> *Although Helen knew her relationship was not healthy, as Matt frequently put her down or ignored her, when he came back from work and gave her a rare compliment, she forgot how mean he was to her and lit up inside. She felt feelings of warmth towards him and a wave of hope about their relationship overtook her. She couldn't help doing this even though, if she was being totally honest with herself, she'd realised that she should be ending the relationship.*
>
> She hadn't been able to do this so far because when Matt was nice to her, he made her feel special and che-

rished, which wasn't the message she'd received as a child. If Helen was to break out of this cycle with Matt, she would have to work on her esteem issues to do with not feeling worthy of being loved.

Camilla had been waiting to hear from Ethan, as he had said he was going to call her during the afternoon. It was now 7pm and she still hadn't heard from him. If she'd let herself, she would have heard her voice of doubt reminding her that this wasn't the first time and that it wasn't just with time-keeping that she couldn't rely on him. How about the times that she asked him to do something for her and he always seemed to forget? What about those occasions when she tried to explain to him what she would like to improve in their relationship and he either didn't listen to her properly, or seemed to and then carried on with the same behaviour as though nothing had been said and agreed upon? And yet when he was being attentive and kind she would've given him the moon... At this point, Camilla buried her thoughts by deciding to fill her time with cooking a great meal. She knew how to win her man!

Here Camilla hid what was bothering her by keeping busy and not thinking about it. Had her self-esteem been better, she wouldn't have stayed in a relationship where her needs were being ignored by someone who wasn't reliable or emotionally available.

The relationships described in both of these examples aren't healthy; with one person becoming a victim and the other acting in a way that wouldn't be acceptable if the people involved had good self-esteem. What's shown here is that neither of the two women (the same applies for men, of course) were able to look at their relationship with objectivity and allow themselves honest conclusions. As they were both dependent on their relationships to make them feel good and valued, the truth of their partner's behaviour was more than they could face. They preferred to continue receiving so little, as it seemed better than having nothing.

What neither of these two women had experienced was what it felt like to have positive self-esteem that came from within them and didn't depend on others to exist. If they'd had this knowledge, they wouldn't have entered into a relationship which wasn't nourishing.

However, all is not lost in these types of relationships. When you work on rebuilding your self-esteem and are no longer reliant on someone else to endorse you, this can be felt in the relationship. If you begin to value yourself and see your worth, the other person can also begin to shift their behaviour and way of being towards you, thereby treating you and the relationship in a more desirable manner. Having stronger self-esteem also leaves you with at least a couple of options (always better than where you were at before!):

a) If the other person also begins to change, your relationship might become properly healthy and you'll have something to work with.
b) As you now rely on yourself to validate your self-esteem, you'll have the inner resources available to end the relationship if that's the solution you choose.

The example below will show you the difference that can be brought to other people's behaviour when you start working on yourself. Up until that point, they have no incentive to change or treat you differently because your lack of self-esteem is almost inviting in this undesirable treatment.

> *Josh had begun to realise that his lack of self-esteem came from his mother withdrawing love from him as a way of manipulating him into doing what she wanted him to. He'd grown up*

fearing that look on her face that showed she wasn't going to give up her unreasonable demands without a fight. Josh had grown used to giving in during these on-going battles as his mother had always shown him approval and affection when he complied with her requests.

When he'd started going out with Faith he hadn't been consciously aware of the fact that she used sulking as a way of getting him to give in and do what she wanted. A deeper part of him had recognised this, however, and it gave him the same feelings as he had had as a child. But Josh was fed up with this controlling behaviour and had decided to join a gym to build up his confidence.

He told Faith what he was doing and why he was doing it. After a few weeks, he was amazed to see that not only did he feel more self-assured, but that Faith had not used sulking and withdrawing as a weapon. She had begun to be more open and less demanding than previously. Their relationship was much stronger as a result.

∞∞∞∞∞∞

And as though this wasn't enough already, here are some other ways that low self-esteem can impact on your wellbeing:

Blame and Guilt

When we have low self-esteem we tend to take things personally and think that a comment is accusatory when it might not be. We find it easy to blame ourselves and to feel guilt, even when the situation doesn't have much to do with us. We could then go on to worry about what's going on, which increases our stress levels and lowers our morale even more, leading to possible depression. When you're in a situation where you feel that you might be apportioned blame or you're taking it for yourself, this is the time to decide to deal with things differently.

> *George listened to what Donna was saying and as she spoke he began to feel guilty, as though he was single-handedly responsible for the fact that they had missed the plane. His toes began to curl as she berated him about his incompetence.*
>
> *This time however, he'd decided that he could no longer accept taking the blame when responsibility should be shared, and so he replied, "I can hear that you're rightfully quite angry about us missing the plane and I'm as bothered about it as you are. However, it makes me feel quite upset that you would take your anger out on me when it's no more my fault than yours. I would prefer that we talked about solutions at this point."*

In acknowledging the feelings that this situation was creating in him, George was able to maintain his self-esteem and wasn't carried into guilt and self-blame as he used to be. He showed that he was aware of his feelings of hurt when he was being wrongfully criticised, but he also took Donna's into account so that they would both feel comfortable about the conversation.

Self-Judgement

We become so used to feeling bad about ourselves that we find ourselves very easily led into self-judgment. We find it so easy to think negatively of ourselves that we can only see our faults, what we do "wrong," what mistakes we make, what our shortcomings are... We also think that others are judging us and that they're not going to like or approve of what they see. This attitude cannot make you view life with hope and anticipation; it will seem very desolate indeed.

Self-Sabotage

Our own self-sabotage will also contribute greatly to diminished self-esteem. The inner critic will be one of the main contributors to this lack of self-worth. If it's constantly reminding you of your flaws and inadequacies, then you're unlikely to feel great about yourself. The result will be that you won't seize the opportunities that life presents to you, either in terms of potential achievements, or on a more personal level of embracing happiness, pleasure and satisfaction. As we've seen in the fourth chapter, it's possible to reframe the thoughts we have about ourselves, and this will permit us to start rebuilding how we think about ourselves and constructing a more positive image.

Self-Sacrifice

As we saw in Chapters 2 and 3, we become a willing partner to our own sacrifice by forgoing our needs and our feelings. We tend to tell ourselves that they're not important and that we don't really have the right to ask to have them met. The outcome of this is that we ignore our honest need for love, kindness, support and recognition, but are willing to give this to others unlimitedly in a bid to gain their approval and appreciation. It's unlikely that you'll ever be properly fulfilled or happy when you're negating your needs and feelings; your self-esteem cannot actively exist when this is the case.

Building Up Your Self-Esteem

Right, well I think we've had enough of looking at how our lack of self-esteem is affecting us. I don't know about you, but feeling miserable used to be my mission in life. Now that I've gotten over myself, I'm never going back there!

Which brings me to the part we've all been looking forward to... *Drum roll, please...*

How do we go about improving our self-esteem and what are the benefits?

Benefits

When you value yourself, you open yourself up to a life that can offer you confidence, contentment and gratification. Be honest with yourself: that does sound a whole lot better than what you've been getting up until now, doesn't it?

- When you're not only aware, but convinced of your value as a human being, it'll have a huge impact on how you go through life. Whereas before you might have hesitated about asking for your needs and feelings to be honoured, now you have no trouble at all doing so, because you know that it's vital for your well-being and you ***DESERVE IT.***
- You'll wave bye-bye to relationships that aren't healthy and which don't fulfil you, or you'll manage them differently so they're less detrimental to you.
- You're no longer into blame, guilt, self-sabotage and the other negative aspects which come as a package when you have low self-esteem.
- You go through life with more confidence in who you are and your abilities. This will automatically influence your expectations and ambitions about what life can bring you.
- You'll have greater resilience to cope with the difficulties that life can bring you as you'll have faith in your ability to cope, but also to trust that it's not personal and that there's better out there waiting for you.
- You'll be less inclined to depression, or to developing an addiction to help you through tough times, or to falling victim to other disorders such as self-harm or eating issues.

But best of all, the one benefit that is the most important is that you will finally **LIKE, nay LOVE** yourself. You'll wake up in the morning in peace and quiet and loving what you see and who you are. Can you get a sense of how that will be?

Improving your Self-Esteem

Recognising that you have low self-esteem isn't another reason to beat yourself up or to give up completely. On the contrary, it's the moment where you start putting your money where your mouth is; where you start initiating change in your life. You've begun this by introducing boundaries. You became aware of the fact that needs and feelings weren't just something that you had to pay attention to and promote in others, but that they were also your right as a human being and that you couldn't live a life of happiness and completion if you weren't respecting them. And then, finally, you silenced your inner critic.

Having already created massive changes like this, the effect on your self-esteem would have been instantaneous. So now there's only one thing left to do to make sure that it all keeps blending smoothly together and forming strong foundations for the new, self-loving you: and that is to adopt the practice of *compassion*.

You won't always get it right, and you won't get it right consistently, at least not at the beginning. But that's **normal**, you're human, and part of life is getting it wrong, making mistakes and losing the beaten track from time to time. Having good self-esteem will allow you to pick yourself back up, brush yourself off and give yourself a massive high five of appreciation before carrying on. The whole point of self-esteem once you've found it again is that it allows you to be gentle and kind and indulgent towards yourself, just as you would towards others. Just think about what that represents for a moment.

Feels wonderful, doesn't it?

How to do it examples

I think that if you've read this far, it's because you want change in your life and you're going to do all you can to make sure that it works. So here's a list to help remind you of what you **don't** want in your life any more:

- Do you always want to be seeing your "flaws" and thinking that others do so too?
- Do you want to live a life in which you anticipate rejection?
- Do you want to be depressed and angry, living in fear of criticism or being undermined?
- Do you want to be scared of trying anything new and missing out on that joy because of your fear of making mistakes and being put down for it?
- Do you want to carry on without proper boundaries, not being able to safely say NO and inviting others to take advantage of you?
- Do you want to live with that feeling in the pit of your stomach because you give more than you should, are always available, and put yourself out for others as a way of "compensating" them for bothering with you?
- Do you want to remain in the shadows because of your anxiety about not being good enough?
- Do you never want to be able to ask for anything because you think you're not worthy and are afraid of being refused?
- Do you want to continue living as though you're a burden to others?
- Do you want to continue not having proper balance and not being valued in your intimate relationships, thinking that you're not likeable or loveable for who you are?
- Do you want the emptiness that not listening to your feelings and needs brings with it?

Do you want to live the whole of your life like that? Aren't you sick of dragging that grey cloud along as a companion?

I'm sure you don't. You're beginning to like yourself way too much for that! So here are some ways to help boost your self-esteem:

> Talk to and about yourself kindly at all times, even if you have to force yourself to begin with. We can all feel the difference between:
>
> *"What's wrong with you? You can't even do that right!"* and *"Oh well, that was a bit of a disaster and not at all what I wanted. Still, at least I tried and I'm learning, so next time it'll be a whole lot better!"*

Or:

> *"You're such a fool, now she's going to tell you to get lost!"* and *"She was out of line and I know it. So I'll explain it to her calmly and kindly but I'm not responsible for her reaction. It's okay to tell someone when you're not feeling respected."*

Or making a decision like:

> *"Rather than saying I'm a big fat dodo and waiting for them to agree, this time I won't invite others to laugh at me. I'll make sure that I only ever speak about myself positively and use complimentary language. I no longer want to put myself down or invite others to view me with derision".*

Here are some other tips for making sure that you safeguard your self-esteem:

- If you're mixing with people who act negatively towards you, then change your crowd and find yourself some friends and activities which are positive and make you feel good. Don't allow yourself to be in contact with people who bring you down (even family members – you can limit your time with them if necessary). Take

pride in what you do and your achievements. Believe in yourself and surround yourself with people who will encourage you and accept you for who you are.
- Find areas where you can make a contribution, as that will do wonders for your self-esteem. It doesn't have to be trekking across the Sahara for charity (perfectionism and critics be damned!), it can be as simple as stopping and helping someone who looks lost, helping your dad to mow his lawn or advising someone with their homework. Anything that makes you feel of value will be good for your self-esteem!
- Acknowledge all the positives about you and about your life. You have a ton of great qualities to recognise now that you know how to go about it. Write them down, as that helps to give you proper proof, and will make you want to keep adding to the list.
- Don't minimise your achievements, and learn to accept compliments when they're given. Don't go looking for them, because that comes from a place of lack, but acknowledge them when they do come and again, if you're with people who don't give you any, then find new people!
- Relax, stop worrying and have fun. The more good times you have, the better you'll feel. The better you feel, the more you'll seek out great times... This is one cycle you won't want to break out of!

∞∞∞∞∞∞

In every respect, self-esteem is the one vital ingredient for a life that is gratifying. I hope that through the chapters of this book, by using the techniques given to establish your boundaries, confirm your needs, listen to your feelings and quiet your critic, you'll have been able to start putting in place the four cornerstones that will uphold your self-esteem. Without them, self-esteem cannot flourish, and without self-esteem, as you will have understood by now, you cannot prosper.

You have just started the greatest journey of your life; I'm sure you can feel it too.

Conclusion

As you'll have seen in the pages of this book, understanding that your way of functioning was more of a coping mechanism brought on by what life had offered you so far will help give you the confidence to realise that you can ditch these habits easily.

That's all they are: habits. ***They don't define who you are.*** You just needed to be aware of how your life, and the events you've experienced, has affected you. Now you can understand the subconscious reactions and responses they created, not only inside you, but also how they coloured your view of the outside world and the people in it. Once that had been explained, you'll surely have seen how effortless it is to detach from these patterns and the rest can become history.

Up until now you might have had a life in which you didn't have proper boundaries and where you were used to denying your feelings and needs. This would have prevented you from giving yourself the information you needed in order to live a life in which you were thriving and felt accomplished. Your mind might've been chaotic, with negative thoughts about yourself and an impaired level of functioning. Who can function well when they're beset with doubt about their value as a human being because of long-held beliefs that impoverish them? When we're not able to be kind and generous to ourselves we set ourselves up for a life in which we're diminished on all levels.

It's only when you're giving yourself what you should always have been receiving that you do well; it isn't selfish at all. For those who weren't used to it, you might have imagined that the world around you would fall apart if you started giving to yourself. If you're a parent, you might've thought that you'd be letting your family down, especially your children. I think by now you'll have realised that, in fact, this doesn't happen, and it's actually a win-win situation for everyone.

Being aware of your own boundaries, needs and feelings means that you're now able to recognise how important they are for you if you want to be doing well. Once that's the case, and you start properly loving and looking after yourself, then you're able to extend this way of being to others and encourage them too. So far from being selfish, you actually become an even kinder and more generous person, as you're better equipped (internally) to do so! You can then move on, and help others to see how important it is that they respect their needs and feelings in a non-needy way. This makes for healthier people and interactions that are balanced and fulfilling.

Stilling the inner critic so that it no longer brings you an endless stream of abuse and put-downs is the next step towards creating a life of abundance for yourself. This isn't possible whilst you're subjected to violence from within. From there, your self-esteem will grow organically; it can't help but respond to care and positive attention. As a result, you'll have found that you're starting to develop self-love. Even if you felt a long way from that at the beginning of this book, you'll have found that it does develop when you start listening to yourself and are respecting what your inner senses are telling you that you require.

The information given in this book is here to serve you as a checklist. If you sense that you're slipping back into modes of behaviour that are detrimental to your well-being, then dive back in for a few moments until you can get yourself back on track. Having spent so many years not receiving the best of what life can offer you, now that you understand why that is, it'll be easy to keep up the momentum you've created!

I hope this book will inspire you to start giving to yourself what every single human being needs and rightfully deserves. You *are* meant to have a life of serenity, fulfilment and intense happiness and can offer it to yourself in a very short amount of time using these five techniques.

I wish you the life you desire: you know how to do it, so now **GO DO IT!**

All the very best,
Amanda

Amanda Butterworth is a psychotherapist and author. She is a mother of three and divorced. She has learnt from her own mistakes and can now share her knowledge with others.

For more information, please refer to Amanda's website:
www.amanda-butterworth.com

Amanda's second book "You got the power" is to be published later on this year. It is an appraisal of society and the influence which it exerts on all of us whether we are aware of it or not. It demonstrates how our capacity for happiness and achievement might have been diminished because of the way society is constructed; and through our uninformed acceptance of this. *"You got the power"* will stimulate your awareness to begin to question those aspects that bind you and which prevent you from expanding as a human and reaching personal fulfillment. It offers you the possibility to find your own answers about what you are genuinely seeking from life. The book gives you the potential to recognize your personal power in all areas and give your life the direction you want it to have.

Introduction

You got the power

(Sample chapter)

What if you were being dishonest with yourself? What if your place in this world and your way of being within it could be very different but you just have no idea that this is even possible? What if you found out that some of the fundamental principles on which you have based your life were inaccurate and you could easily change them? What if your self-growth had been stunted without you realizing because of the ideas which have received, and which have formed who you think you are and what you can expect from life. If you explored them properly you might find that you don't connect with them as closely as you might originally have thought. If you readjusted them, you really could start living a life which made you truly happy and properly fulfilled in all its aspects; relationships, jobs, personal satisfaction, the realization of dreams and ambitions...

I can hear you now; you probably think I'm crazy. After all you can't be that deluded about your life? You probably think that life is life; you take it as it is, the good and the bad, but you can't change anything essentially. You might agree that you can personally control or influence certain areas of your life, but that overall there's nothing you can necessarily do about the affect the big old world out there has on you and your life. After all, if society and our communities are structured the way they are, it must be because that it is the way it has been thought through and they are at their most advantageous for the majority of us. If our close environment has developed as it has, it is in order to adapt to the basic nature of us, the human being. We are shown and advised that if there is any flourishing to do, we will do it in these surroundings.

But what if there were another way? What if just by changing a few basic beliefs about yourself and this world in which you find yourself, your experience of life could be completely different? If you were able to let go of what you have been told about how the world operates and what you can expect to get from it; would you not then discover that certain limitations which you had felt were imposed upon you by society and by yourself, had suddenly been lifted? Would you not automatically find that there was now potentially so much more out there waiting for you that you could dare seek?

If your vision of the world were changed, it literally could transform how you feel about yourself and what you believe about your life and what it has to offer. It could offer you the peace, tranquility, satisfaction and love to which all human beings would naturally aspire. Somehow we expect life to not always be easy, to not necessarily give us what we would like and overall to not be the fulfilling experience it could be.

Why is this?

And what if this weren't truly the case?

Would you be quick to reject that idea, so firm is your belief in your vision of the world and your place in it? You would probably say that our experiences are subjective and our conclusions are our own, so your vision would be based upon seasoned fact. Would you confirm that you do not feel the need to question your environment and its structure because you are satisfied that is couldn't really be any other way? Are you certain that your potential for achievement and happiness has been encouraged at all times; or at least as much as opportunity allowed? Do you believe that society fulfils its contract towards you and others and promotes your well-being? So many questions we all could have...

Is this the truth of it?

Most of us do seem to go about our business, very accepting of the circumstances in which we find ourselves. We are unlikely to challenge the way of things. Through what we are taught and have presented to us, we have accepted that things are as they are because that is their natural order. We become accustomed to the ideas and principles which are suggested to us and live with the expectation that in following this framework, things will work out for the best. After all, others have been before us and tested many different blueprints and scenarios for how to live successfully both in our immediate environment and within the wider society. Society itself has had its fair amount of reorganizing. If this is the order of our world as we find it, it must inevitably be the one most suited to our requirements.

And yet, if that is the case, how is it that so many of us are not doing well in societies that have the luxury of doing more than mere surviving? Why it is that most of us are becoming increasingly overcome by the trials of life and the ever more meager expectations which we have of it. Why is it that basic aspects of life which should be simple and easy so often do not seem to be that way? There is an ever growing struggle to get it all done, get the job, get the money, get the security, get the house, get the life... But what happened to your life? Did you ever get it, have you got it now?

What is this myth we are sold about ourselves and other people; about our surroundings and our world? Where is this life of contentment and plenty that is seemingly, tantalizingly just around the corner? Does this not sometimes feel like an illusion; and a fairly uncomfortable one at that? Surely you must at some stage have had a moment of doubt; a time when you queried what was going on and how come you didn't ever seem to get to where you thought you were going; the goalposts always appear to move.

Have you not had moments when you allowed yourself to acknowledge that life was sometimes painful, only occasionally rewarding, infrequently fulfilling? Some of you may feel that this is indeed the case on a frequent basis; but the sense of overwhelm these feelings provoke discourage you from being able to address the situation. However, many others of you will feel this only sporadically, as transient phases of your life from which you emerge not too stunned, not too shocked... not feeling any urgency to focus on the problems and sort them out in order to cancel the need for a further rerun. Still others will have lives with which they are on the whole more than satisfied, but where perhaps one aspect might need evaluating and as such the need is not pressing and can be suppressed.

We choose to let these disruptive problems and circumstances slide. Who has the time, who has the energy to attend to them when so often we seem to be engulfed by this frenzied, never ending race on the treadmill that life has become. Without being consciously aware of it, we allow ourselves to be suspended in a semi-permanent state of tepidness, with infrequent highs. If we have paid some attention to these events and feelings, it is unlikely that we have had the time to stop and do so properly. But actually it is more probable that we have not consciously questioned the conditions in which we all find ourselves. This is what "we" do, this is what our peers do, this is what "people" have always done and so we accept this state of being as an integral part of life; that's apparently just *how it is*.

But what if that weren't necessarily the case? What if your life could be completely different? What if it were possible to have the lifestyle and the ease without the pain and stress? It sounds very idealistic doesn't it and you could perhaps say that it seems more than a little absurd. After all if there's one thing we're aware of, it's what we have to do and put up with in order to have a certain kind of life. In fact that's what we've been told and experienced often in our lives! We all know that it doesn't come easy and it's not for those who want to stay in bed all day; get with the programme!

And that perhaps is the crux of it; the programme, or rather the programming. If you haven't ever actually stopped to ask yourself what it is that *you* want, what it is that *you* like, what it is that makes *you* truly happy (and I'm not talking about fleeting moments of pleasure) then how do you know if what you're living is what you have chosen rather than some version you've accepted because of what you've been taught and come to expect?

What if we were able to consciously look at what we've been told, possibly for the first time in our life and decide which parts we choose to believe and want to keep, and which do not serve us in any way other than to make us potentially feel terrible most of the time? How would it feel to be inspired to have a totally new point of view of your life circumstances; one you wouldn't have begun to imagine was even possible?

Would you not want to be able to say that you have evaluated and sensed who you are; that you have seen what your "real" hopes and dreams are and to know that you can move towards and ultimately achieve them?

So I'm asking you now, as you're reading this book, what do you LIKE about your life, what are the parts that you accept as unavoidable, and which bits do you quite frankly HATE?

You may find it difficult to answer those questions. Or you might find them so disagreeable you're just going to keep your head down and keep going because taking the lid off that whole can of worms might be a big mistake. Or perhaps you think that it would be pointless to even ask because you are just one tiny little cog in a very oily engine which you couldn't even begin to change if you wanted to. The most you can do is grease yourself up as best you can and try and slip and slide through 'til the end.

So I'll ask you this, what about those moments when you just KNOW that you're really not *"lovin' it"*? They do come, you know they do. What happens inside you when they blip in out of nowhere?

And now for the crunch question, the one which might make you squirm: **who are you**? And no, I'm not asking you to give me your perceived identity. I'm enquiring as to who you are in the depths of you. Can you answer, or does it start to make you feel uncomfortable. Is it excruciating, are you beginning to feel tense, or cross or attacked?

I'm sorry if I've caused you annoyance or distress, but sometimes we need a little bit of discomfort because that is what makes us sit up and take note. When it's all going smoothly we tend to just glide on unthinkingly for as long as the ride lasts. So? I apologize for being so persistent, but were you able to answer?

This is a book about society, its constructs and your recognized function within it. You might not yet be aware of the real influence and limiting effect which society and your close environment has had on you personally and what you find in your life. *"You got the power"* will present information and alternatives which will allow you to query those beliefs you might currently hold about yourself and the place you occupy. I believe it will encourage you to change your perception of certain received ideas and assumptions, in particular those which do not serve you. I hope it will help you reevaluate so that you can now consciously begin choosing those aspects which suit you as opposed to adapting yourself to fit them. I hope you will be able to see yourself and your environment in a different light, one which will open many doors for you.

This is possible. It is not a foolish dream and there are people out there who can confirm that it is achievable and it works. I am one of those people. I have walked where you walk now; I did so for over 30 years. It didn't occur to me that anything other than what I was living as the sometimes forbidding reality of my life could exist; there was apparently no alternative. I know what it feels like to accept that your current situation is your fate. There might also be many other contributing factors, such as familial responsibilities and financial obligations which now make it seem even less likely that change is either sensible or possible. You might feel convinced that you actually enjoy some or most of what fills your life. But what if there were more? What if your life could change and get even better?

My wish for you is that if you weren't able to answer the question about "who you are", the true you, then you soon will be able to. The material which will be presented to you in the pages of this book will assist you in doing that. It will help you get to a place where you will have started to be back in touch with the real you in a way which it would not have occurred to you to even imagine. You will realize that you might have been living a form of life in which you had very little real connection with yourself and that which made you feel vibrantly alive.

Up until now you might, without knowing it, have been living under the influence of a multitude of endorsements and instructions from outside yourself which have quietly stunted your potential. You might well have adopted them unquestioningly as your own. I am going to suggest that you look within and find your own answers, your truth; what works for you once you have let go of the doubt and the fear which often accompanies us when we feel we are stepping out and braving it; alone.

To realize yourself, you have to realize who you are.

When you have reconnected with your real Self a whole world of potential and change will open up to you. Please believe me; you can lead your life to where you want it to be. No mini revolution involved, no dropping of everything and moving to the other side of the world, no drama. Just good old fashioned common sense and decisions made with an open, knowing mind. You will rediscover information which has always been available to you but which has been entombed within your psyche and which is no longer instinctively accessible. It is possible to change your life; dare I even say it, maybe even effortless to do so?

Your life will at last give you the ease and joy of which you might only have had momentary glimpses up until now. You will be able to have a life of contentment and fulfillment, with happiness a daily constant, not an occasional high.

This is what I will bring you with this book. It is a manual for change, but it is not a self-help book; it is a *self-serve*.

Printed in Great Britain
by Amazon